PIANO / VOCAL / GUITAR

MOVIE SONGS

Exclusive Distributors:
Music Sales Limited
8/9 Frith Street, London W1D 3JB, England.
Music Sales Pty Limited
120 Rothschild Avenue, Rosebery, NSW 2018, Australia.

Order No. HLE90001934
ISBN 1-84449-109-9

Printed in the USA

Your Guarantee of Quality
As publishers, we strive to produce every book to the highest commercial standards.
The book has been carefully designed to minimise awkward page turns and to make playing from it a real pleasure.
Throughout, the printing and binding have been planned to ensure a sturdy, attractive publication which should give years of enjoyment.
If your copy fails to meet our high standards, please inform us and we will gladly replace it.

www.musicsales.com

Hal Leonard Europe
Distributed by Music Sales

CONTENTS

ALFIE

Theme from the Paramount Picture ALFIE

Words by HAL DAVID
Music by BURT BACHARACH

Dm7
Dm7/G
Cdim7
Dm7/G
Are we meant to take more than we give, or are we meant to be kind?
G13
G9♯5
2 fr
3 fr
C(add9)
Dm7/G
And if on-ly fools are kind, Al-fie, then I
Cmaj7
Cmaj6/9
Em7
A7
Dm7
guess it is wise to be cruel. And if life be-longs on-ly to the strong,
Em7
Am7
Dm7
Dm7/G
Cdim7
Al-fie, what will you lend on an old gold-en rule? As

Bm7 Eb6/D Am7/D

sure as I be - lieve there's a heav - en a -

Bm7 Am7/D Bm7

bove, Al - fie, I know there's some - thing much

Eb6/D Am7/D Dm7/G G9 G13 2fr G9

more, some - thing e - ven non - be - liev - ers can be - lieve in.

C(add9) Dm7/G F#m7b5 F9

I be - lieve in love, Al - fie. With - out true love we just ex -

Em7
Am7
F#m7♭5
F9
ist, Al - fie. Un - til you find the love you've
Em7
Am7
D9#11
4fr
Dm7/G
missed you're noth - ing, Al - fie. When you walk let your heart
rall.
l.h.
a tempo
F#dim7
Dm7/G
lead the way, and you'll find love an - y day,
rall.
C7♭9
Dm9
C7♭9
Cmaj9
Cmaj7
Al - fie, Al - fie.
dim. poco a poco
pp

ALL FOR LOVE

from Walt Disney Pictures' THE THREE MUSKETEERS

Words and Music by BRYAN ADAMS,
ROBERT JOHN "MUTT" LANGE and MICHAEL KAMEN

D/A
be there when _ you're old, to have and _ to
from the wind and _ the rain, from the hurt and _
When hon - or's _ at stake, this vow I ____ will
1
A
hold. When there's love in - side _ pain.
2,3
A
make:
D Dsus/E D/F#
N.C.
Let's make it
that it's
G
all for one and all for love. ______
Em7
D/A
Let the one you hold be the one you want, the one you _

A
D/F#
G
Bm
A
D/F#
G
need, 'cause when it's all for one it's one for all. When there's
Em7
D/F#
G
D/A
some - one that should know then just let your feel - ings show and make it
G
D/F#
Em7
A
To Coda
D
D.S. al Coda
all for one and all for love. When it's love you make
CODA
D
Bm
Don't lay our

G
Em7
D/F♯
G
A
love to rest 'cause we could stand up to the test. We got
Bm
D/F♯
ev - 'ry - thing and more than we had planned,
G
A
Bm
more than the riv - ers that run the land.
D/F♯
G
A
We've got it all in our hands.

G
Em7
Dsus
D
Dsus
D
G
Em7
Asus
A
N.C.
Now it's all for one and all for love.
G
Em7
(It's all for love.)
Let the one you hold be the one you

D/A
A
D/F#
G
Bm
A
D/F#
want, the one you need, 'cause when it's all for one it's one for all.
G
Em7
D/F#
G
D/A
(It's one for all.) When there's some-one that should know then just let your feel-ings show. When there's
Bm7
2fr
D/F#
G
D/A
Em7
some-one that you want, when there's some-one that you need let's make it all, all for one
Gm
3fr
Gm7
3fr
Asus
D
and all for love.
a tempo

ALMOST PARADISE

Love Theme from the Paramount Motion Picture FOOTLOOSE

Words by DEAN PITCHFORD
Music by ERIC CARMEN

Em7
D
C
G(add9)/B
G/B
se - cre - cy. I faced the nights a - lone. (Both:) Oh,
rain - y day, they're fin - 'lly com - ing true. (Both:) I'll
C
G(add9)/B
G/B
C
G/B
B/D♯
4 fr
how could I have known that all my life I on - ly need - ed you?
share them all with you, 'cause now we hold the fu - ture in our hands.
Em
G/D
C
C/D
D
Gsus4(sus2)
G
D/G
G
Oh, al - most par - a - dise. We're knock-ing on
cresc.

D/E
Em7
D/E
Em7
Gsus4(sus2)
G
D/G
G
heav - en's door. _
Al - most
par - a - dise. _
How
D/E
Em
Em/D
C
Am
could we ask _ for ___ more?
I swear that I __ can see __ for - ev - er
C/D
D7
C/G
G
To Coda
in
your ___ eyes.
Par - a - dise. __
Em9
Em
D/C
C/D
Gsus4(sus2)
G
dim

E♭
C
(Male:) And in your arms, salvation's not so far away.
D.S. al Coda
E♭
C/D
D
C/D
D
It's getting closer. (Both:) Closer ev'ry day. Almost
CODA
Em9
Em
D/C
C/D
C/G
G
Paradise.
D/E
Em
Am/C
D
C/G
G
G(add9)
Paradise.
dim.
8vb

AMERICAN PIE

from THE NEXT BEST THING

Words and Music by
DON McLEAN

Em
Am
Em
Am
But Feb-ru-ar-y made me shiv-er with ev-'ry pa-per I'd de-liv-er.
C
G/B
Am
C
D
Bad news on the door-step I could-n't take one more step I
G
D/F#
Em
Am7
D
can't re-mem-ber if I cried when I read a-bout _ his wid-owed bride,
G
D/F#
Em
C
D7
G
C
Some-thing touched me deep in-side ____ the day the mu-sic died. ____

Moderately
G
G
C
G
D
So bye - bye, Miss A - mer - i - can Pie Drove my
G
C
G
D
Chev - y to the lev - ee but the lev - ee was dry. Them
G
C
G
D
To Coda
good ole boys were drink - in' whis - key and rye Sing - in'
Em
A7
this - 'll be the day that I die,

Em D7

This - 'll be the day that I die.

G Am

1. Did you write the book of love and do you
2.-4. *See additional lyrics*

C Am Em

have faith in God a - bove? If the Bi - ble tells

D G D/F#

you so Now do you be - lieve in

Em
Am7
C
rock and roll. __ Can mu - sic save your mor - tal soul __ and
Em
A7
D
can you teach me how to dance_ real slow? ______
Em
D
Well, I know that you're_ in love with him __ 'cause I __
Em
D
C
G
__ saw you danc - in' in the gym, __ You both kicked off __ your shoes._

A7
C
D7
Man, I dig those rhy - thm and blues. I was a
G
D/F♯
Em
Am
lone - ly teen - age bronc - in' buck with a pink car - na - tion and a
C
G
D/F♯
Em
pick - up truck. But I knew I was out of luck the day
C
D7
G
C
the mu - sic died.

1,2,3
4
G D7 G D7 G C
I start-ed sing-ing He was sing-in' bye - bye, Miss A-
G D G C G D
mer-i-can Pie Drove my Chev-y to the lev-ee but the lev-ee was dry. Them
G C G D
good ole boys were drink-in' whis-key and rye Sing-in'
Em A7 Em
this-'ll be the day that I die, This-'ll be the day that I

D7
die.
rit.
Freely
G
D/F♯
Em
Am
C
I met a girl who sang the blues and I asked her for some hap - py news, But
Em
D
she just smiled and turned a - way.
G
D/F♯
Em
G
Am
G/B
C
I went down to the sa - cred store where I heard the mu - sic years be - fore But the

Em C D
man there said the mu - sic would - n't play. And
Em Am Em Am
in the streets the chil - dren screamed, the lov - ers cried and the po - ets dreamed. But
C G/B Am C D G D/F♯ Em G/B
not a word was spo - ken the church bells all were bro - ken. And the three men I ad - mire most, the
C D7 G D/F♯ Em
Fa - ther, Son and the Ho - ly Ghost, They caught the last train for the coast the

Additional Lyrics

2. Now for ten years we've been on our own,
And moss grows fat on a rollin' stone
But that's not how it used to be
When the jester sang for the king and queen
In a coat he borrowed from James Dean
And a voice that came from you and me
Oh and while the king was looking down,
The jester stole his thorny crown
The courtroom was adjourned,
No verdict was returned
And while Lenin read a book on Marx
The quartet practiced in the park
And we sang dirges in the dark
The day the music died
We were singin'... bye-bye... etc.

3. Helter-skelter in the summer swelter
The birds flew off with a fallout shelter
Eight miles high and fallin' fast,
it landed foul on the grass
The players tried for a forward pass,
With the jester on the sidelines in a cast
Now the half-time air was sweet perfume
While the sergeants played a marching tune
We all got up to dance
But we never got the chance
'Cause the players tried to take the field,
The marching band refused to yield
Do you recall what was revealed
The day the music died
We started singin'... bye-bye... etc.

4. And there we were all in one place,
A generation lost in space
With no time left to start again
So come on, Jack be nimble, Jack be quick,
Jack Flash sat on a candlestick
'Cause fire is the devil's only friend
And as I watched him on the stage
My hands were clenched in fists of rage
No angel born in hell
Could break that Satan's spell
And as the flames climbed high into the night
To light the sacrificial rite
I saw Satan laughing with delight
The day the music died
He was singin'... bye-bye... etc.

THEME FROM ANGELA'S ASHES

Paramount Pictures and Universal Pictures International Present ANGELA'S ASHES

Music by
JOHN WILLIAMS

mp
cresc.
mf legato

mp
(♪ = ♪)
mf
mp
mf
3
3
3
3
3

Reflectively
mp
With motion
mf
f
mf
f
mf
3
5
ff
mf
mp
Moderately
mf

Original tempo
rit.
p

3
6
rit.
Freely
pp
8vb

AS TIME GOES BY

Words and Music by
HERMAN HUPFELD

Dm
Dm7
G7
C
Em
Am
Dm
mat-ter what the prog-ress, or what may yet be proved, The sim-ple facts of life are such they
Liltingly
Dm7/A
Fm6/A♭
G7sus
G7
Dm
G7
Gm6
G7
can-not be re-moved. You must re-mem-ber this, a kiss is still a kiss, a
rit.
a tempo
C
G+
C6
Em
Am
Em/G
D7
sigh is just a sigh; The fun-da-men-tal things ap-
G7sus
G7
Dm7
G7
Cmaj7
C6
Cmaj7
C6
ply, As time goes by. And

Dm7 G7 Gm6 G7 C G+ C6 Em
3fr
3fr
when two lov - ers woo, they still say, "I love you," On that you can re - ly;
Am Em/G D7 G7sus G7 Dm7 G7
No mat - ter what the fu - ture brings, As time goes
C F Dm7♭5 C C7 F
by. Moon - light and love songs
A7/E Dm F♯dim7
nev - er out of date, Hearts full of pas - sion, jeal - ous - y and hate;

Am/E F7 D7 G7 Gdim7
Wom - an needs man ___ and man just have his mate, That no one can de -
poco rit.
G7 Dm7 G7 Gm6 G7
ny. It's still the same old sto - ry, a fight for love and glo - ry, A
a tempo
C G+ C6 Em Am Em/G D7
case of do or die! The world will al - ways wel - come
C C♯dim Dm7 G7 G7♯5
1 C Am D7 G7
2 C B♭7 C
lov - ers, As time goes by. You by.

BABY ELEPHANT WALK

from the Paramount Picture HATARI!

Words by HAL DAVID
Music by HENRY MANCINI

B♭
F
R.H.
B♭
F

C
B♭
F
f
N.C.
B♭
F
B♭
F
N.C.
mp
f
B♭
mf
F
C
mp

B♭
F
mf

B♭

F

C
B♭
F
Very slowly
F7
F13♯11
f
mp
Ped.

BECAUSE

from AMERICAN BEAUTY

Words and Music by JOHN LENNON
and PAUL McCARTNEY

1.
2.
Ddim
Tacet
Ddim
Tacet
F♯
2. Be–
Love is old, love is new;
love is all, love is
G♯7
D.S. al Coda
you.
3. Be–
Coda
D
Ddim
Ah
C♯m
D♯m7♭5
G♯7
A
Ah
C♯m
A9
A13
D
Ddim
Oo
Ah.
4fr
5fr

BORN TO BE WILD

E♭
G♭
A♭
E♭
make it hap - pen, take the world in a love em - brace.
G♭
A♭
E♭
G♭
A♭
Fire all of your guns at once and ex - plode in - to space.
1
E♭
B♭
2
E♭
Like a true na-ture child we were born,
G♭
A♭
born to be wild. We have climbed so high,

G♭
E♭
D♭
nev - er want to die.
Born to be wild.
E♭
D♭
E♭
D♭
Born to be wild.
E♭
D♭
1
2
E♭
D♭
E♭
D♭
Repeat and Fade
Born to be wild.

COME SATURDAY MORNING
(Saturday Morning)
from the Paramount Picture THE STERILE CUCKOO

Words by DORY PREVIN
Music by FRED KARLIN

Ebsus
Ab
Db
C7sus
Sat - ur - day spend till the end of the day.
Sat - ur - day laugh more than half of the day.
Fm
C7sus
Fm
Bb
Just I and my friend.
Just I and my friend.
Fm
C7sus
Fm
Bbsus
Bb9
Bb7
Bb9
Bb7
Ebmaj7
We'll trav - el for miles in our Sat - ur - day smiles,
dressed up in our rings and our Sat - ur - day things,
Amaj7
Ab
Gm7
and then we'll move on.

Ab
Gm
Cm
Fm7
Fm9
But we will re - mem - ber long af - ter
Bb9
Bb7
Eb
Bb7sus
Eb
Ab
Ab6
Sat - ur-day's gone.
Come Sat - ur - day Morn - ing.
1.
Eb
Eb7sus
Eb
Ab
Ab6
Come Sat - ur - day Morn - ing.
2.
Eb
Bb7sus
Eb
Ab
Ab6
Repeat and fade
Come Sat - ur - day Morn - ing.

THE CRYING GAME

from THE CRYING GAME

Words and Music by
GEOFF STEPHENS

C
G
Em
is to know a - bout the cry - ing game.
Bm
C
Em
I've had my share of the cry - ing game.
C
Solo ends
First there are kiss - es,
C+
F
then there are sighs, and then, be - fore you

Eb
3fr
Bb
D
To Coda
know where _ you are, you're say - ing good - bye. ___
N.C.
One day _ soon, I'm gon - na tell the moon _ a - bout the
G
A
C
G
Em
cry - ing game. _
Bm
C
And if he knows, _ may - be

Em
C
he'll ex - plain
why there are
C+
heart-aches,
why there are tears,
F
E♭
3fr
B♭
D
and what to do to stop feel - ing blue when love dis - ap - pears.
D.S. al Coda
CODA
B
Don't want no more

F#
of the cry - ing game. I
A
E
don't want no more of the cry - ing game.
1
2
B
Oh!

DIAMONDS ARE A GIRL'S BEST FRIEND

from GENTLEMEN PREFER BLONDES

Words by LEO ROBIN
Music by JULE STYNE

Gm7 C7 F
pen - sive jew-els;
keep their flick-er;
a tempo
Chorus
C7 F Bb F C7
A kiss on the hand may be quite Con - ti - nen - tal But
There may come a time when a lass needs a law - yer, But
F Fdim Gm6 C9b C7 D7 Gm
Dia-monds Are A Girl's Best Friend,
A kiss may be
Dia-monds Are A Girl's Best Friend,
There may come a
D7 G Am7 Gdim G Am7 G7
grand But it won't pay the rent-al on your hum-ble flat
Or
time When a hard boiled em - ploy - er thinks you're aw ful nice,
But

C9 Gm7 C9 C7 F9 Fdim F9 B♭ A
help you at the Au - to - mat. Men grow cold as girls grow
get that "ice" or else no dice. He's your guy when stocks are
mp
B♭ B♭dim F A7 Dm G7 C7 F C7
old And we all lose our charms in the end. But
high, But be - ware when they start to de - scend. It's
F Cm6 Am7 D7 Gm7
square - cut or pear - shape, These rocks don't lose their shape, Dia - monds Are A
then that those lous - es Go back to their spous - es, Dia - monds Are A
cresc.
C9♭ F Fdim C7 F C7 F B♭6 F
Girl's Best Friend. A
Girl's Best Friend.
f
mf
f

THE DREAME
from SENSE AND SENSIBILITY

By PATRICK DOYLE

I am un - done to - night. Love, in a sub - tle dreame dis -
guised, hath both my heart and me sur - prised,
whom nev - er yet he durst at - tempt a - wake. Nor will he tell me for whose
sake he did me the de - light or

spight, but leaves me to in - quire in all my wild de - sire of
sleep a - gain, who was his aid, and sleep so guil - tie
cresc.
and a-fraid, and since he dares not come with - in
my sight.

EVERYBODY'S TALKIN'

(Echoes)

from MIDNIGHT COWBOY

Words and Music by
FRED NEIL

Gm7
C7
F
I'm go - in' where the sun keeps shin - in' thru the pour - in' rain,
F7
Gm7
C7
go - in' where the weath - er suits my clothes.
F
F7
Gm7
Bank - in' off of the
C7
F
F7
north - east wind, sail - in' on a sum - mer breeze,

B♭ C7 F

skip-pin' o-ver the o-cean like a stone.

D.S. al Coda

CODA

And

C7

I won't let you leave my love be-hind.

F

Repeat and Fade

And

EIGHTEEN WITH A BULLET

from LOCK, STOCK & TWO SMOKING BARRELS

Words and Music by
PETE WINGFIELD

F Dm7 Gm7 C11

got my fin-ger on the trig - ger,___ I'm gon-na pull it.

F C/D Dm7 Gm9 C11

I'm hit to click now,_ I'm a son-of-a-gun,___ huh.

To Coda ⊕

F C Dm7 Gm9 B♭dim7

So hold it right there lit-tle girl,___ we gon-na have big fun, lis-ten.

Am7 A♭dim7 Gm7 C11

I may be_ an old-ie,_ but I'm a good-ie too._

E♭dim7
Gm7
B♭m6
I will last forever baby and I'll be good oh,
F/C
1.
C11
oh yes I will, ha!
2.
C11
Dmaj9
never babe, ooh.
Instrumental
Em7/D
Dmaj9
Em7/D
We got a

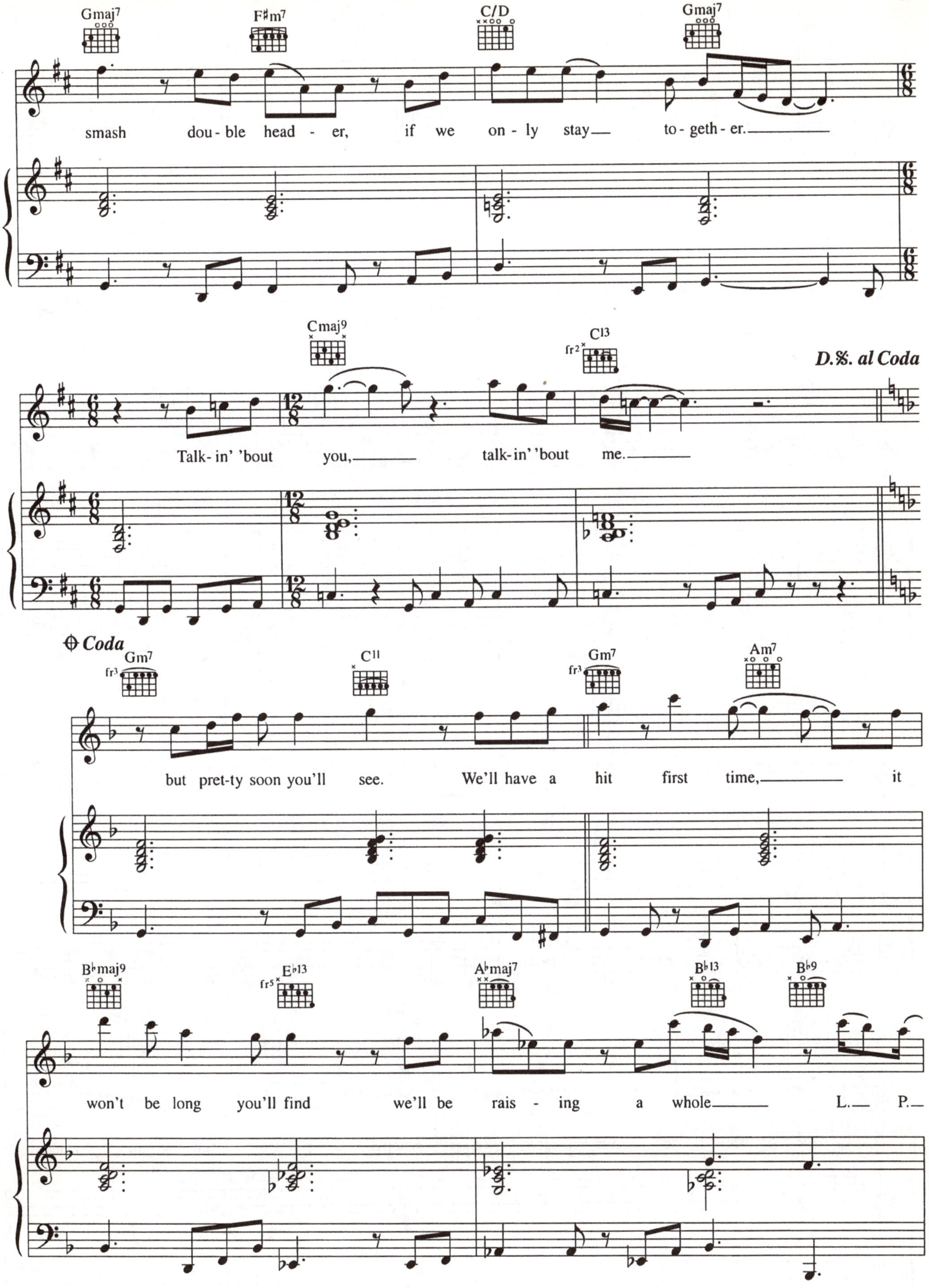

Gmaj7 F♯m7 C/D Gmaj7

smash double header, if we only stay together.

Cmaj9 C13 *D.𝄋 al Coda*

Talk-in' 'bout you, talk-in' 'bout me.

𝄌 Coda

Gm7 C11 Gm7 Am7

but pret-ty soon you'll see. We'll have a hit first time, it

B♭maj9 E♭13 A♭maj7 B♭13 B♭9

won't be long you'll find we'll be rais - ing a whole L. P.

E♭11
A♭maj9
Fm7
Ah hey,
B♭m7
E♭11
A♭maj9
Fm7
ha, you know that I'm ready, oh yes, for
B♭m7
E♭11
A♭maj9
Fm7
you, oh baby. I'm tipped for the top, I ain't
B♭m7
Edim7
Cm7
Edim7
never, never gonna stop until I'm

A♭maj9 Fm7 B♭m7 E♭11

in your heart ba - - - - by, yeah.

Repeat ad lib. to fade

A♭maj9 Fm7 G♭maj9 Edim7 Cm7 Edim7

Long as we stay with each other.

Verse 2:
I'm eighteen with a bullet
Got my finger on the trigger
I'm gonna pull it.
I'm a super soul sureshot, papa
I'm a national breakout
So let me check your playlist, baby
Come on, and let's make out.

I'm high on the chart
I'm tipped for the top
Until I'm in your heart
I ain't never gonna stop
Never, baby.

Verse 3:
I'm eighteen with a bullet
Got my finger on the trigger
I wanna pull it, huh
Be my 'A' side, baby
'B' side me
Right now I'm a single
But pretty soon you'll see.

THE FIRM – MAIN TITLE

from the Paramount Motion Picture THE FIRM

By DAVE GRUSIN

8va
8va
E♭/F
f
8va

Gm7
mf
8va
8va

8va
D♭/B
B♭/C
f
8va

A♭/B♭
8va
8va
8va
Gm7
mf
8va
3

8va
8va
8va
8va
3
mp

8va
(♪ = ♪)

GOD GIVE ME STRENGTH

from GRACE OF MY HEART

Words and Music by ELVIS COSTELLO
and BURT BACHARACH

F♯sus4
F♯7
Bm
Bm/A
G
still break. And I don't have an-y-thing to share,
(3º vocal)
Bm7
Esus4
E7
A
that I won't throw a-way in-to the air.
G
A
Em7
That song is sung out. This
A
Em7
F♯m7
bell is rung out. She was the light that I'd

A Em7 F♯m7 A

bless, she took my last chance of hap - pi - ness. So

Gm9 fr3 Bm7 A/B Bm7 Em7 *To Coda* ⊕

God give me strength, God give me

1. D Gmaj7 Em7 A7sus4 N.C.

strength.

2. D Gmaj7 Em7 A13 fr5

grant me her in - dul - gence and de - cline, I might as well

wipe her from my me-mo-ry.
Frac - ture the spell as
Bm
E/G♯
fr2
she be-comes my e-ne-my.
May - be I was washed out like a
Aadd9
Bm
E/G♯
fr2
A
Bm
A/C♯
lip print on his shirt.
See I'm on-ly hu-man, I want him to
3
A13
fr5
D.%. al Coda
hurt.
I want him,
I want him to

Verse 2:
I can't hold on to her
God give me strength.
When the phone doesn't ring
And I'm lost in imagining
Everything that kind of love is worth
As I tumble back down to the earth.

That song is sung out *etc.*

Verse 3 **D.%.**:
Instrumental 14 bars
Since I lost the power to pretend
That there could ever be a happy ending.

That song is sung out *etc.*

THE FRIENDSHIP THEME

from Touchstone Pictures' BEACHES

Music by GEORGES DELERUE

rall.
Ped.
*

GIRL TALK

from the Paramount Picture HARLOW

Words by BOBBY TROUP
Music by NEAL HEFTI

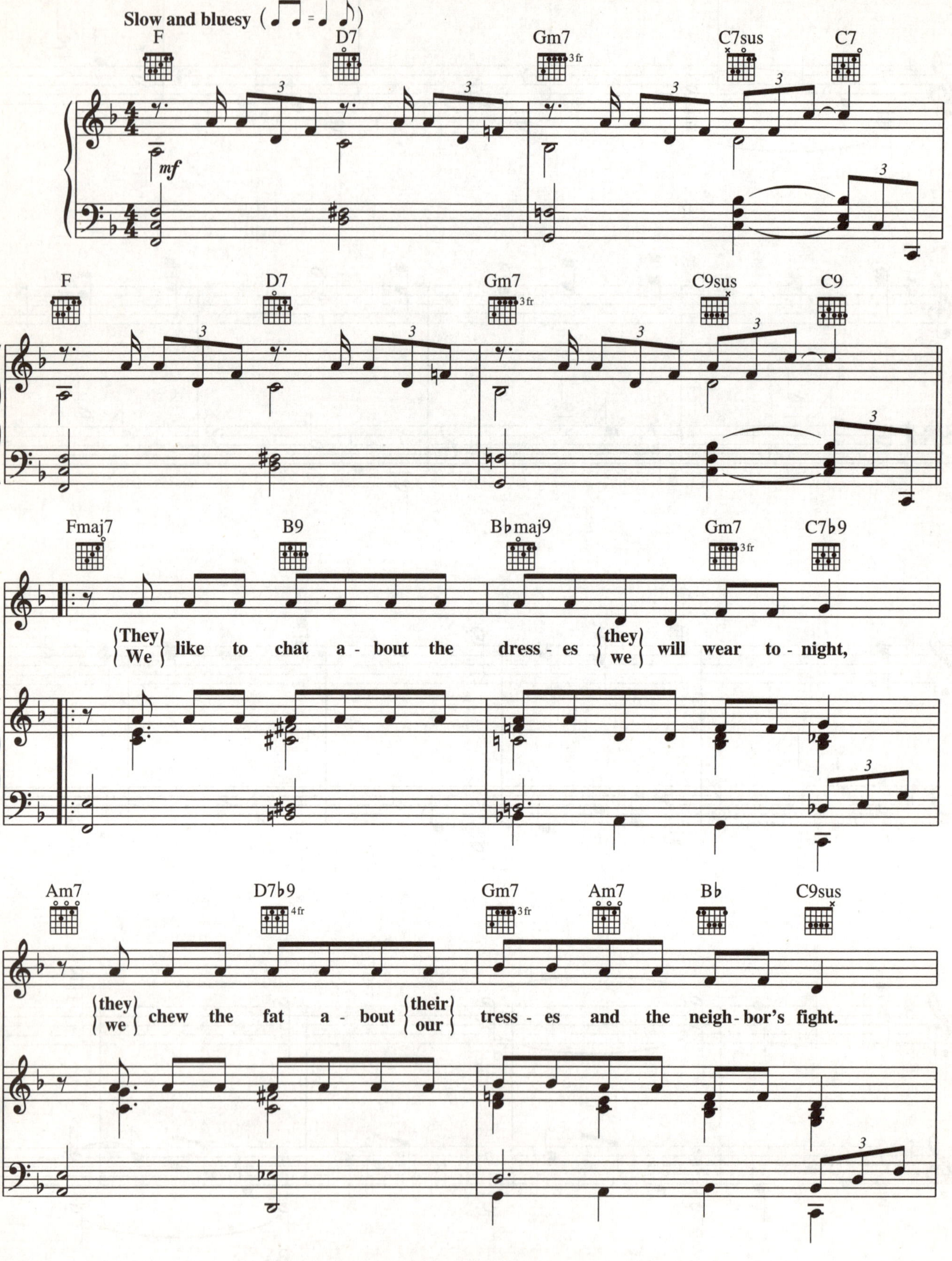
Slow and bluesy
F D7 Gm7 3 fr C7sus C7
mf
F D7 Gm7 3 fr C9sus C9
Fmaj7 B9 B♭maj9 Gm7 3 fr C7♭9
{They / We} like to chat a - bout the dress - es {they / we} will wear to - night,
Am7 D7♭9 4 fr Gm7 3 fr Am7 B♭ C9sus
{they / we} chew the fat a - bout {their / our} tress - es and the neigh - bor's fight.

Fm7
B♭m7
G7♭5(♭9)
Gm7/C
C7♭9
In - con - se - quen - tial things that men don't real - ly care to know
Am7
D7♭9
4 fr
Am7
B♭m
Cm6
D7
be - come es - sen - tial things that wo - men find so "ap - pro - po".
Dm7/G
G9
Gm7/C
B♭m7
But that's a dame, {they're / we're} all the same it's just a game. {They / We} call it
Am7
Dm9
Gm7
3 fr
C9
Girl Talk, Girl Talk.

Fmaj7
B9
B♭maj9
Gm7
C7♭9
They / We all me - ow a - bout the ups and downs of all their / our friends,
Am7
D7♭9
Gm7
Am7
B♭
C9sus
the "who", the "how", the "why", they / we dish the dirt, it nev - er ends.
Fm7
B♭m7
G7♭5(♭9)
Gm7/C
C7♭9
The weak - er sex, the speak - er sex we / you mor - tal males be - hold,
Am7
D7♭9
Am7
B♭m
Cm
D7
but tho' we joke we would - n't trade you for a ton of gold.

Dm7/G
G9
Gm7/C
B♭m7
So ba - by stay and gab a - way, but hear me say that af - ter
(It's all been planned, so take my hand, please un - der-stand the sweet - est
Am7
Dm9
Gm7
C7♭9
Girl Talk, talk to
Girl Talk talks of
F
D7
Gm7
C9sus
C9
me.
you.)
F
Am7
B♭maj9
Bm7♭5
C9sus
Fmaj9
me.
you.)
8va

GO THE DISTANCE

from Walt Disney Pictures' HERCULES

Music by ALAN MENKEN
Lyrics by DAVID ZIPPEL

D E F♯m A/C♯ Dmaj7 Esus E D E A
great warm wel-come will be wait - ing for me. Where the crowds will cheer when they
D E F♯sus F♯m D C♯ F♯m
see my face, and a voice keeps say - ing this is
mf
Dmaj7 Esus E A/C♯ Bm/D
where I'm meant to be. I will find my way.
A/E E E/D A/C♯ Bm/D
I can go the dis - tance. I'll be there some - day

A/E
E
E/D
A/C#
Dsus2
F#m7
if I can be strong. I know ev - 'ry mile will be worth my
Bm7
2 fr
D
E
A
A/G#
F#m
F#m/E
Dmaj7
while. I would go most an - y - where to feel like
Esus
E
A
E/A
D/A
I be - long.
lightly
poco rall.
a tempo
mp
A
E/A
D/A
D
E
A

D
E
A
D
E
F♯m
Dmaj7
Esus
E
simply
D
E
A
D
E
F♯sus
F♯m
R.H.
D
C♯
F♯m
Dmaj7
Esus
E

Dsus2/F#
E/G#
A
E/A
D/A
poco rall.
a tempo
7
A
E/A
D/A
F
G
C
mf
F
G
C
F
E
Am
Fmaj7
f
Gsus
3 fr
G
F/A
G/B
C/F
G7
C/E
Dm/F
I am on my way.

C/G G G/F C/E Dm/F C/G G G/F
I can go the dis - tance. I don't care how far, some-how I'll be strong. I know
C/E F Am7 Dm7 C/E
ev - 'ry mile will be worth my while. I would
F G C G/B Am C/G Fmaj7 Gsus G C G
go most an-y-where to find where I be - long.
poco rall.
a tempo
C G F G C5
3 fr
rall.
p

GODZILLA – MAIN THEME

(Opening Titles)

from the TriStar Motion Picture GODZILLA

Written and Composed by
DAVID ARNOLD

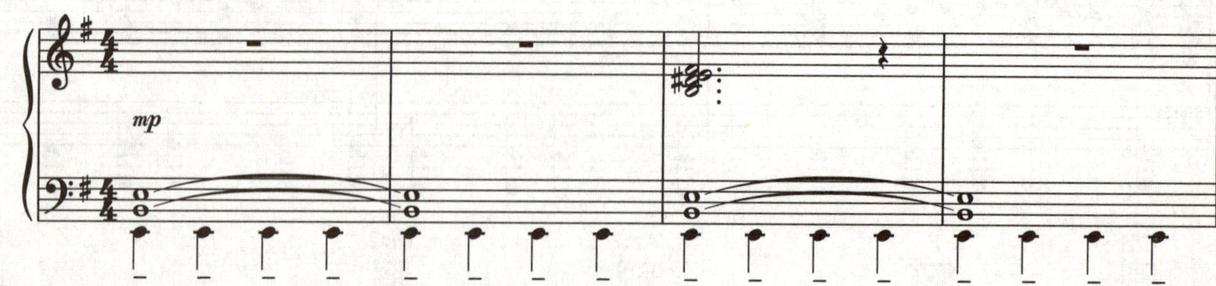

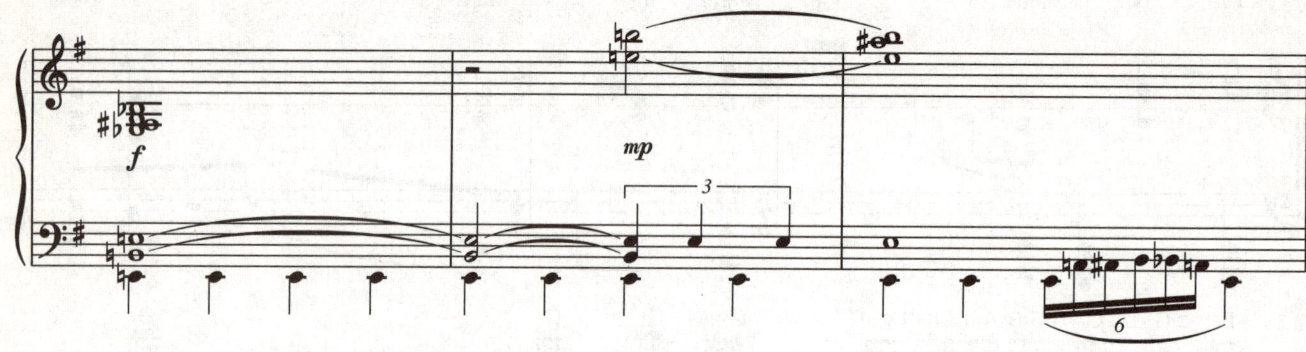

f
R.H.
ff
fff
tremolo
Urgently
ff

3
3
3
3
3
3
3
3
3
3
3
3
3
3
3
3
f
mf
mp

GOTHAM CITY

from BATMAN AND ROBIN

Words and Music by
ROBERT KELLY

F♯
C♯
B
how loud, qui - et nights in the midst of crime.
how child - ren are drown - ing in their tears.
F♯
C♯
B
How next door to hap - pi - ness lives sor - row and
How we need a place where we can go, and
D♯m
C♯/E♯
F♯
sig - nals of so - lu - tion in the sky.
then when ev - 'ry - one will have a he - ro
A ci - ty of just -
C♯
B
- ice, a ci - ty of love, a ci - ty of peace

F♯
C♯
B
F♯
C♯
for ev - 'ry-one of us.
We all need it,
can't live with-
B
D♯m
C♯/E♯
F♯
1.
out it,
Goth - am
Ci - ty,
oh
yeah.
2.
C♯
A ci - ty of just - ice,
a ci - ty of love,
B
F♯
C♯
a ci - ty of peace
for ev - 'ry - one of us.

B
F♯
C♯
B
'Cause we all need it, can't live with-out it, Goth-am
D♯m
C♯/E♯
F♯
B
C♯/A♯
Ci-ty, oh yeah.
Yet in the mid-dle of storm-y
G♯m7
fr4
F♯
Fm7
B♭7
E♭m
/D♭
wea-ther, we won't stum-ble and we won't
E♭m/C
G♯m7
fr4
C♯
D
fall. I know a place that of-fers shel-ter. Ci-ty of just-

G D C
- ice, a ci - ty of love, a ci - ty of peace
G D C G D
for ev - 'ry-one of us. We all need it, can't live with-
C Em D/F♯ G
1, 2.
out it, Goth - am Ci - ty, oh yeah. Ci - ty of just -
3.
Fadd9 C/E G
Repeat ad lib. to fade
Goth - am Ci - ty, (ev - 'ry - bo - dy go.) Goth - am
(Don't you want to go.)

GOLDFINGER

from GOLDFINGER

Words and Music by JOHN BARRY,
LESLIE BRICUSSE and ANTHONY NEWLEY

C C7 F D♭
A spi-der's touch. Such a cold fin-ger
Fmaj7 F B♭
beck-ons you to en - ter his web of
E Am Am+5 Am6 Am+5
sin. But don't go in. Gold-en
Em B7 Em
words he will pour in your ear, but his lies can't dis - guise what you

B7♯9
E
Cm
fear. For a gold - en girl knows when he's kissed her.
Gm6
D♭°
F
B♭
it's the kiss of death from Mis - ter Gold - fin - ger.
Fmaj7
F
B♭
Pret - ty girl, be - ware of this heart of
E
1.
Am
Am+5
Am6
Am+5
gold. This heart is cold. Gold-en

2.
Am Am+5 Am6 Am+5 Am Am+5
cold. He loves on - ly gold,
Am6 Am+5 Am Am+5 Am6 Am+5 Am Am+5
on - ly gold. He loves gold.
Am6 Am+5 Am Am+5 Am6 Am+5 Am Am+5
He loves on - ly gold, on - ly gold.
Am6 Am+5 Am Am+5 Am6 Am+5 Am6 9
He loves gold, he loves gold.

THEME FROM "GOODBYE, COLUMBUS"

from the Paramount Picture GOODBYE, COLUMBUS

Words and Music by
JAMES YESTER

Em
Cmaj7
Bm
It's a luck - y day 'cause I found you. Gon - na build a new
Fmaj7
Bm
Fmaj7
F7
world a-round you. Touch the sun and run. It's a luck - y day.
Dsus
G/D
G
Hel - lo life. Good -
Em
Bm
Fmaj7
- bye, Co-lum - bus. I got a feel-in' that you're gon - na hear from us.

Bm
Em
B♭maj7
Fmaj7
You're gon - na know that we've tak - en the world by sur - prise.
B♭
E♭maj7
3 fr
D
Got that look in our eyes. It's a luck - y day
Gmaj7
Cmaj7
Fmaj9
just for chang - in', leav - in' the old world be - hind.
B♭maj7
Gmaj7
Cmaj7
Luck - y day for walk - in' the new road

Fmaj9
B♭maj9
Am
just to clear your mind.
It's a day for
Bm
Cmaj7
Em/B
Bm
Em/B
start-in' a new way,
tell-in' the old one good-bye.
Am
Bm
Cmaj7
Luck-y day
for get-tin' a-bove it.
Spread your wings and
Fmaj7♯11
Dsus
D.S. and Fade
fly.

A GUY WHAT TAKES HIS TIME

from SHE DONE HIM WRONG

Words and Music by
RALPH RAINGER

G
F7
So I've
E♭7
G
thought it out and there is - n't a doubt, my con - clu - sion is all for the
F♯7
G
G♯dim
D7
G♯dim
D7
G♯dim
D7
best. I need some - one who can sup - ply com-fort and some rest.
G
A

G G+ Em G+ G G+ Em G+
guy what takes his time, I'll go for an - y - time. __ I'm __ a
guy what takes his time, I'll go for an - y - time. __ A has - ty
G G+ Em G+ G G+ Em G7
fast mov - in' gal who likes 'em slow. __ Got __ no
job real - ly spoils the mas-ter's touch. __ I __ don't
C Cm Am7♭5
use for fan - cy driv - in', want to see a guy ar - riv - in' in low. __
like a big com-mo - tion, I'm a de - mon for slow mo - tion or such. __
G G+ Em G+ G G+ Em G♯dim D7 G♯dim
I'd __ be sat - is-fied, e - lec - tri - fied to
Why __ should I de - ny that I would die to
3fr
4fr

D7
G
know a guy what takes ___ his time. ___
know a guy what takes ___ his time. ___
D7
G
G+
3fr
Em
G+
3fr
A hur - ry - up af - fair, I
There is - n't an - y fun in
G
G+
3fr
Em
G+
3fr
G
G+
3fr
Em
G+
3fr
al - ways give the air. ___ Would - n't give an - y rush - in' gent a smile. _
get - tin' some-thin' done ___ if ___ you're rushed when you have to make the grade. _
G
G+
3fr
Em
G7
C
Cm
3fr
___ I ___ could go for an - y sing - er who would
___ I ___ can spot an am - a - teur, ap - pre - ci -

Am7♭5
G
G+
Em
G+
G
G+
Em
G♯dim
con - de-scend to lin - ger a - while. What _ a
ate a con - nois-seur at his trade. Who _ would
D7
G♯dim
D7
lul - la - by would be sup-plied to have a guy what takes ___ his time. _
qual - i - fy, no al - i - bi, to be the guy what takes ___ his time. _
1 G
D7
A
2 G
F7
E♭7
D♭7
G

HAVE YOU EVER REALLY LOVED A WOMAN?

from the Motion Picture DON JUAN DeMARCO

Words and Music by BRYAN ADAMS, MICHAEL KAMEN and ROBERT JOHN LANGE

Cm
3fr
fly. Then when you find your-self ly - in' help - less in her
Dsus
D
Dsus
D
𝄋 only
C/G
C/D
3
arms, ya know ya real - ly love,
C/G
C/D
G
G/D
G
love a wom - an. When you love a wom - an you
D
tell her that she's real - ly want - ed. When

D9
4fr
G
you love a wom - an you tell her that she's the one,
G/F#
Em7
Edim
she needs some-bod - y to tell her that it's gon - na last
Am7
D9
4fr
Am7
D7
Am7
D9
4fr
for - ev - er.
So tell me have you ev - er real - ly,
3
3
To Coda
Am7
D7
G
1
N.C.
3
real - ly real - ly ev - er loved a wom - an?
2. To real - ly love a
3

2
E♭
3fr
You got to give her some faith. hold her tight: a lit-tle
G
D7
ten - der - ness, you got-ta treat her right. She will be there for you
G
D.S. al Coda
tak-in' good care of you. (Ya real-ly got-ta love your wom - an, yeah.)
CODA
G
Am7
D9
4fr
wom - an? Just tell me have you ev-er real - ly,

Additional Lyrics

2. To really love a woman, let her hold you
 Till ya know how she needs to be touched.
 You've gotta breathe her, really taste her.
 Till you can feel her in your blood.
 N' when you can see your unborn children in her eyes.
 Ya know ya really love a woman.

 When you love a woman
 You tell her that she's really wanted.
 When you love a woman
 You tell her that she's the one.
 Cuz she needs somebody to tell her
 That you'll always be together
 So tell me have you ever really,
 Really really ever loved a woman?

3. *Instrumental*

 Then when you find yourself
 Lyin' helpless in her arms.
 You know you really love a woman.

 When you love a woman *etc.*

I SAY A LITTLE PRAYER

featured in the TriStar Motion Picture MY BEST FRIEND'S WEDDING

F♯m7
B
say a lit - tle prayer for you.
say a lit - tle prayer for you.
say a lit - tle prayer for you.)
Em7
Am7
While comb - ing my hair now, and won - d'ring what
At work, I just take time, and all through my
D
Gmaj7
F♯m7
dress to wear now,
cof - fee break time,
I say a lit - tle prayer for you.
End solo
B
C
D/C
For - ev - er, for - ev - er, you'll

Bm7
2 fr
G/B
F/G
G
C
D/C
stay in my heart and I will love you. For - ev - er and ev - er, we
Bm7
2 fr
G/B
F/G
G
F/G
G
C
D/C
nev - er will part. Oh, how I'll love you. To - geth - er, to - geth - er, that's
Bm7
2 fr
G/B
F/G
G
C
D/C
3
how it must be. To live with - out you would on - ly mean heart - break for
B
1
2
To Coda
D.S. al Coda
me.

CODA
Em7
Am7
My dar - ling, be - lieve me,
C/D
for me there is no one but
Gmaj7
Am7/D
Gmaj7
you. Please love me, too.
Am7/D
Gmaj7
Am7/D
I'm in love with you, an - swer my

Gmaj7
Am7/D
Gmaj7
prayer.
Say you love me, too.
Am7/D
Gmaj7
Why don't you an - swer my prayer?
Am7/D
Repeat and Fade
You know, ev - 'ry day I say a lit - tle

I WANT TO SPEND MY LIFETIME LOVING YOU

from the TriStar Motion Picture THE MASK OF ZORRO

Music by JAMES HORNER
Lyric by WILL JENNINGS

A♭m7
to the end. Seize the day, stand up for the
B♭
light.
E♭m
Both: I want to spend my life - time
B♭
lov-ing you
E♭m
if that is all in life I
B♭
ev - er do.
Male: He - roes rise,

E♭m/B♭
he - roes fall. __ Rise a - gain, win it all. ______
A♭m7
4fr
B♭
Female: In your heart, _ can't you feel the glo - ry? ________
E♭m/G♭
E♭m
Through our joy, through our pain, _ Both: we can move worlds a - gain. ____
A♭m
4fr
B♭
Take my hand, ________ dance _ with me. Male: Dance _ with me. Both: I want to

E♭m
B♭
spend my life - time lov-ing you if that is
noth - ing else to see me through if I can
1
E♭m
B♭
all in life I ev-er do. I will want
2
A♭m
4fr
B♭
spend my life - time lov-ing you.
3
G♭
D♭
B♭m

Ebm
Bb
Bb/Ab
Gb
Db
Male: Though we know we will nev - er come a - gain,
Bbm
Ebm
where there is love,
Both: life be -
Bb
Ebm/Bb
Abm6
4fr
Bb
gins o - ver and o - ver a - gain.

E♭
3fr
A♭m/C♭
A♭
4fr
Save the night, save the day. Save the love come what may.
D♭m
4fr
E♭
3fr
Love is worth ev-'ry-thing we pay. I want to
A♭m
4fr
E♭
3fr
(1.,2.) spend my life - time lov-ing you
(3.) noth - ing else to see me through
1,2
A♭m
4fr
if that is all in life I
if I can

E♭
3 fr
ev - er do.
I want to
I will want
3
D♭m7
spend my life - time
loving you.
A♭m/E♭
4 fr
p
Slower

IF I WERE A RICH MAN

from The Musical FIDDLER ON THE ROOF

Words by SHELDON HARNICK
Music by JERRY BOCK

Cm
D7
G7
To Coda
C
Guitar Tacet
bid-dy, bid-dy rich,
dig-guh, dig-guh, dee-dle dai-dle
man. I'd build a
rall.
Quasi rubato
Fm
Bb7
Ebmaj7
Bbm6
C7
big tall house with rooms by the doz-en, Right in the mid-dle of the town; A
Fm
G7
C
C7
fine tin roof with real wood-en floors be-low. There could be
Fm
Bb7
Ebmaj7
Bbm6
C7
one long stair-case just go-ing up and one e-ven long-er com-ing down; And

Fm
F♯dim
G7
C7
one more lead - ing no - where just for show.
I'd fill my
rall.
F
G7
C
A7
yard with chicks and tur - keys and geese And ducks for the town to see and hear;
Dm7
G7
C
C7
Squawk - ing just as nois - i - ly as they can.
And each loud
Fm
B♭7
E♭maj7
B♭m6
C7
quack and cluck and gob - ble and honk Will land like a trum-pet on the ear;
As
(imitate sounds)

Fm
F#dim
G7
D.S. al Coda
if to say here lives a wealth - y man.
(Sigh)
rall.
Quasi rubato
CODA
C
Guitar Tacet
Fm
Bb7
man. I see my wife, my Gold - e, look-ing like a rich man's
Ebmaj7
Bbm6
C7
Fm
G7
wife with a prop-er dou-ble chin; Su - per - vis - ing meals to her heart's de -
C
C7
Fm
Bb7
light. I see her put-ting on airs and strut-ting like a pea - cock

Ebmaj7
Bbm6
C7
Fm
F#dim
Oy! What a hap-py mood she's in. Scream-ing at the ser-vants day and
G7
C7
Rubato
night. The most im-por-tant men in town will come to fawn on_ me;
Fm
Db
They will ask me to ad-vise them,__ Like Sol-o-mon the wise, "If you
Bbm
C7
please, Reb Tev-ye, par-don me, Reb Tev-ye." Pos-ing prob-lems what would cross a rab-bi's eyes.

Freely
Deliberately (in tempo)
Fm7
Bb7
Boi, boi, boi, boi, boi, boi, boi, boi, boi.
And it won't make one bit of dif - f'rence
Ebmaj7
Bbm6
C7
Fm
F#dim
If I an - swer right or wrong?
When you're rich, they think you real - ly
G7
C7
Reflective
F
G7
know.
If I were rich, I'd have the time that I lack, To
rall.
p
C
A7
Dm7
G7
sit in the syn - a - gogue and pray;
And may - be have a seat by the east - ern

C
C7
Fm
Bb7
wall.
And I'd dis - cuss the ho - ly books with the learn - ed
Ebmaj7
C7
Fm
F#dim
G7
men sev - en ho - urs ev' - ry day;
This would be the sweet - est thing of all.
Tempo I
C
(Sigh)
If I were a rich man,
Dai - dle, dee - dle, dai - dle, dig - guh, dig - guh, dee - dle, dai - dle,
G7
Cm
D7
dum.
All day long I'd bid - dy, bid - dy bum,
If I were a wealth - y

G7
C
man. Would-n't have to work hard, Dai-dle, dee-dle, dai-dle dig-guh, dig-guh, dee-dle, dai-dle,
8va
Rubato
G7
Cm
G7
dum. Lord, who made the li-on and the lamb, You de-creed I
8va
Cm
G7
Cm
A7-5
D7-5
G7
should be what I am; Would it spoil some vast e-ter-nal plan, If I were a wealth-y
15ma
8va
C
G7
C
man?
8va
a tempo
8va

IL POSTINO
(The Postman)
from IL POSTINO

Music by LUIS BACALOV

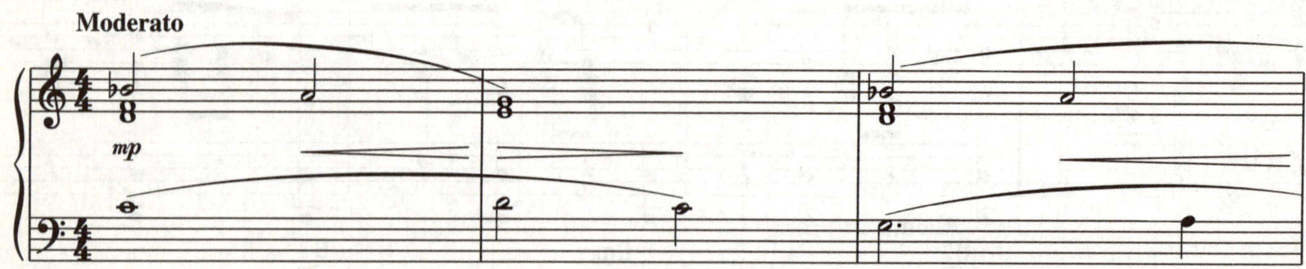

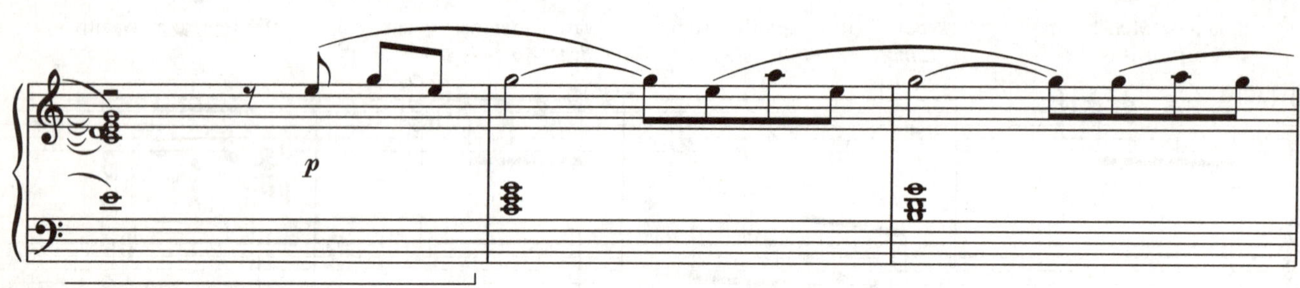

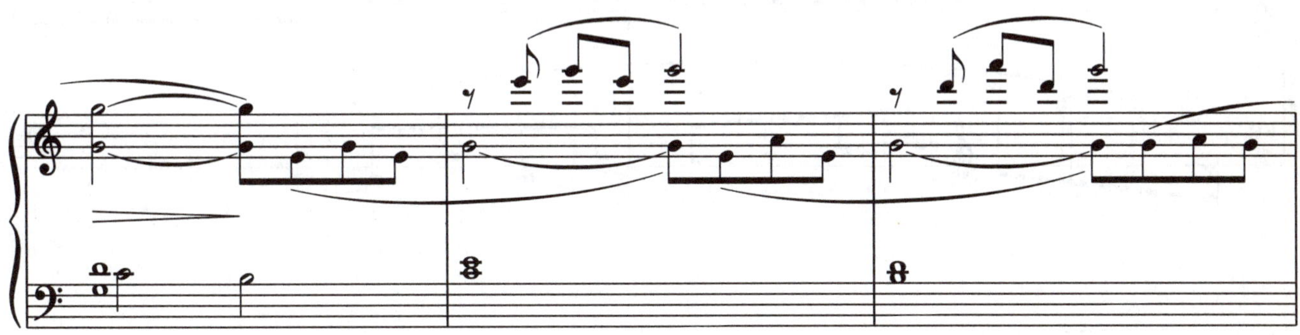

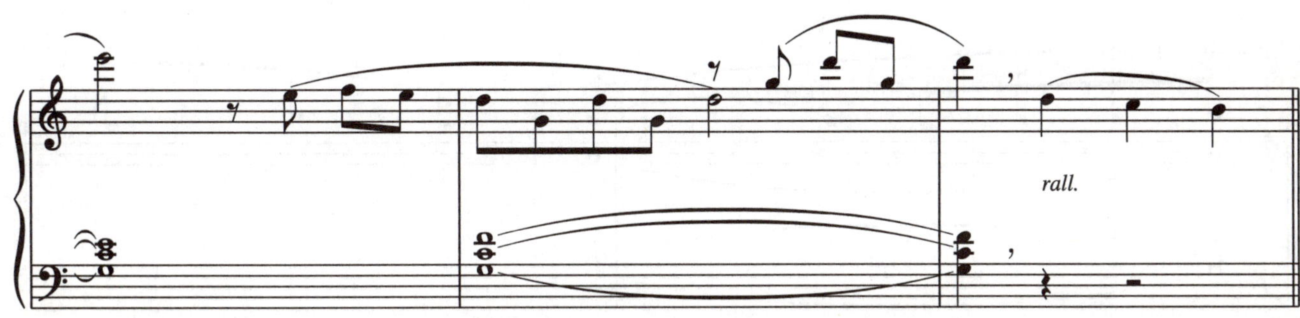
rall.

Mosso
p
rall.

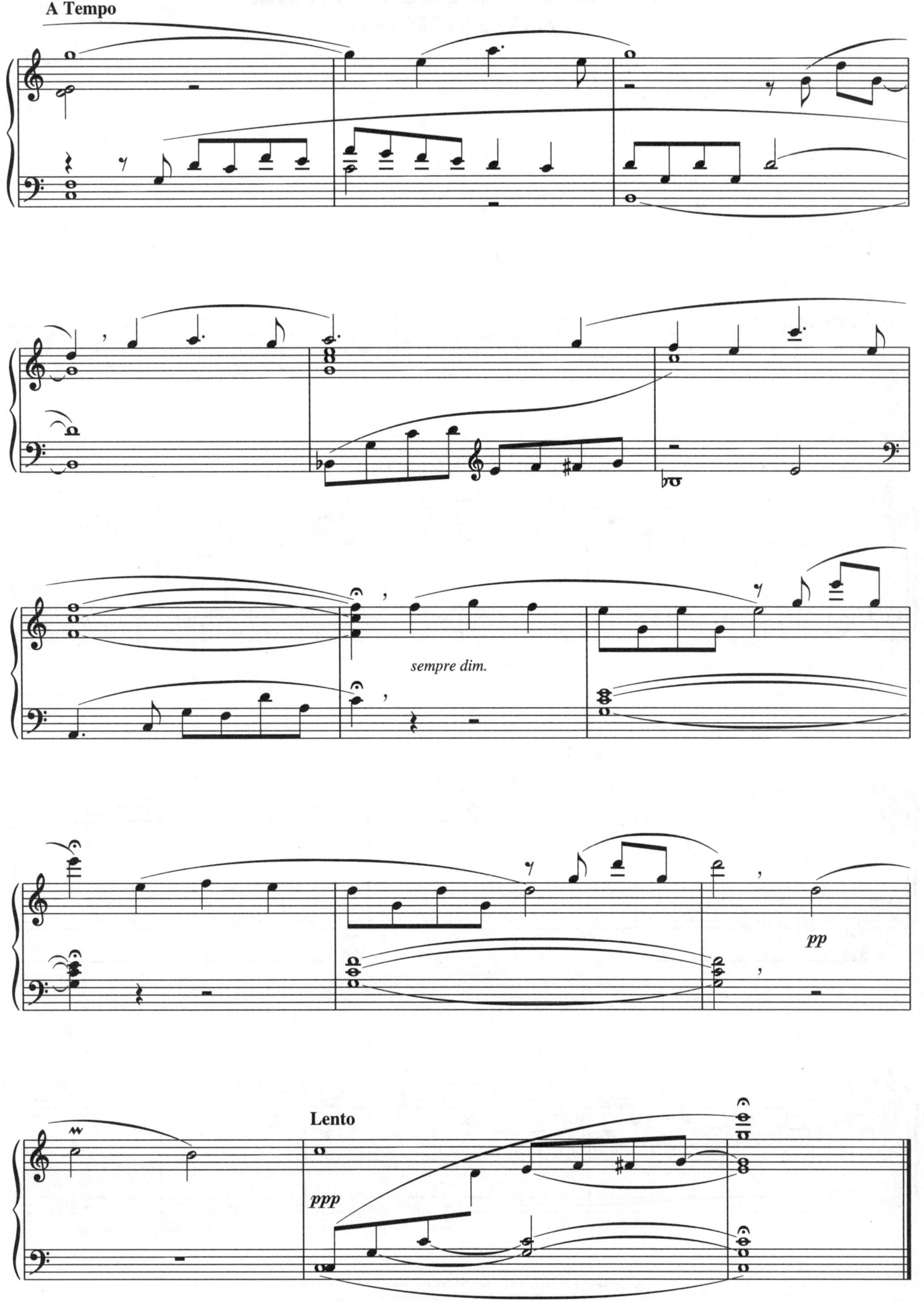
A Tempo
sempre dim.
pp
Lento
ppp

THE IPCRESS FILE

from THE IPCRESS FILE

By JOHN BARRY

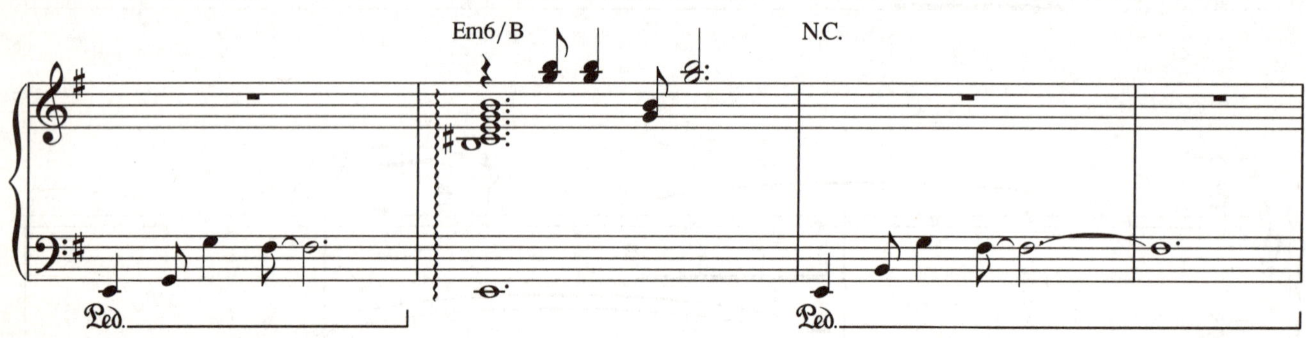

Em6/B
Em6
Em6
Am7
B
Bm7(♭5)
Am6
B aug
Em6
Am7
C♯7

To Coda
Am6
B7
Em6
C6
F#7
Fm6
B7
D.S. al Coda
Coda
Em6
rit.

IT'S A LIFE

from the Paramount Motion Picture THE TRUMAN SHOW

By BURKHARD DALLWITZ

cresc.
f

JAILHOUSE ROCK

from THE BLUES BROTHERS

Words and Music by JERRY LEIBER
and MIKE STOLLER

D7
Eb7
Chorus
gan to swing._ You should have heard those knocked - out jail - birds sing. Let's
Ab7
4fr
Eb7
rock! Ev - 'ry - bod - y let's rock!
To Coda
Bb7
Ab7
4fr
Ev - 'ry - bod - y in the whole cell block was danc -
1-3
Eb7
D7
4
Eb7
- ing to the Jail - house Rock! - ing to the Jail - house

Additional Lyrics

2. Spider Murphy played the tenor saxophone
   Little Joe was blowin' on the slide trombone.
   The drummer boy from Illinois went crash, boon, bang;
   The whole rhythm section was the Purple Gang.
   (Chorus)

3. Number Forty-seven said to number Three:
   "You're the cutest jailbird I ever did see.
   I sure would be delighted with your company,
   Come on and do the Jailhouse Rock with me."
   (Chorus)

4. The sad sack was a-sittin' on a block of stone,
   Way over in the corner weeping all alone.
   The warden said: "Hey, Buddy, don't you be no square,
   If you can't find a partner, use a wooden chair!"
   (Chorus)

5. Shifty Henry said to Bugs: "For heaven's sake,
   No one's lookin', now's our chance to make a break."
   Bugsy turned to Shifty and he said: "Nix, nix;
   I wanna stick around a while and get my kicks."
   (Chorus)

KISSING YOU

from WILLIAM SHAKESPEARE'S ROMEO + JULIET

Words and Melody by DES'REE
Music by TIM ATACK

Dm7
Am7
G/B
C
G/B
Am
C/G
watch - ing stars with-out you, My soul cried:
Dm7
Cadd9
C
Am
Em7
Am
C/G
Heav - - - ing heart is full of pain.
Dm7
Am7
G/B
C
G/B
G♯dim
Am
Oh, oh, the ach - ing! 'Cause
Dm7
Am7
G/B
C
G/B
Am
C/G
I'm kiss - ing you, oh.

Dm7 Am7 G/B C G/B Am C/G
I'm kiss - ing you, oh.
Dm7 Cadd9 C Am Em7 Am C/G
Touch me deep, pure and true; A
Dm7 Am7 G/B C G/B Am C/G
gift to me for - ev - er. 'Cause
Dm7 Am7 G/B C G/B Am C/G
I'm kiss - ing you, oh.

Dm7
Am
G/B
C
G/B
Am
C/G
I'm
kiss - ing you, oh.
Dm
C
Am
G add 2
p poco a poco cresc.
etc.
Dm
C
Am
G add 2
F
G
Am
G/B
Dm9
fr3
Dm7
C
G/B
Am
rit.
Yeah,
yeah,
yeah.
ff

a tempo
Dm7
Am7
G/B
C
G/B
Am
C/G
Where are you now? Oh,
p
Dm7
Am
G/B
C
G/B
Am
C/G
where are you now? 'Cause
Dm7
Am
G/B
C
G/B
Am
C/G
I, oh, I'm kiss - ing you.
Dm7
Am
G/B
C
G/B
Amadd9
Am
molto rit.
I'm kiss - ing you, oh.

THEME FROM "LAWRENCE OF ARABIA"

from LAWRENCE OF ARABIA

By MAURICE JARRE

D
Cm
3 fr
D
E♭
D
Cm
D
Fm
Gm
Cm
poco accel.
cresc.
D
Cm
D
f a tempo
mp
B♭
E♭dim7
B♭
A♭m6
4 fr
B♭
C♭
A♭m
f
Cdim7
B♭
Bdim7
F9
B♭
E♭dim7
B♭
A♭m6

B♭
C♭
B♭
A♭m6
4 fr
B♭6
D♭m
4 fr
E♭m
A♭m
4 fr
B♭
A♭m
4 fr
B♭
F7
B♭
E♭dim7
B♭
A♭m6
4 fr
B♭
A♭m6
4 fr
B♭
F7
B♭
Cdim7
B♭
Cdim7
ff
f
mf
rall.
mp
p
B♭
With fire
A♭m
4 fr
B7♭5
B♭
ff
molto rit.

LES POISSONS

from Walt Disney's THE LITTLE MERMAID

Lyrics by HOWARD ASHMAN
Music by ALAN MENKEN

Am7 D9 Am7 A#dim7 G/B
pull out their bones. Ah mais oui, ca c'est tou - jours de - lish.
D7 G Gmaj7 G6
Les pois - sons, les pois - sons, hee hee hee, hah hah hah.
G G7 C
With the clea - ver I hack them in two. I pull
C C#dim7 G/D E7
out what's in - side and I serve it up fried. God, I

Am
D7
G
love lit - tle fish - es, don't you?
Here's
E♭
B♭7
E♭
B♭7
E♭
some - thing for tempt - ing the pal - ate,
Pre - pared in the
B♭7
E♭/G
E♭
Gm/D
clas - sic tech - nique.
First you pound the fish flat with a
C7
B♭/F
B♭+
B♭6
mal - let.
Then you slash through the skin, give the bel - ly a

B♭/A♭
E♭/G
D7
slice, then you rub some salt in 'cause that makes it taste
rit.
G
Gmaj7
G6
nice. Sa - cre bleu! What is this? How on earth could I
Gmaj7
G
G♯dim7
Am7
D7
miss such a sweet lit - tle suc - cu - lent crab. Quel dom -
Am
Am♯7
Am7
D7
mage. What a loss. Here we go in the sauce. Now some

Am7
A#dim7
G/B
D7
G
flour — I think, just a dab. Now I stuff you with
Gmaj7
G6
G
G7
bread. It don't hurt 'cause you're dead. And you're cer - tain - ly luck - y you
C
C6
Cmaj7
C#dim7
G/B
are. 'Cause it's gon - na be hot in my big sil - ver
E7
Am7
D7
G
pot. Too - dle loo, mon pois - son, au re - voir!

LEGENDS OF THE FALL

from TriStar Pictures' LEGENDS OF THE FALL

Composed by JAMES HORNER

F♯m C♯m G D F♯m C♯m G D
mf
simile
F♯m C♯m C G Bm F♯m G A
rit.
Tempo I
D Bm G A D
Bm C Em Bm G
A D Bm G A7 Bm
rit. e dim.

A LIFE LESS ORDINARY

from A LIFE LESS ORDINARY

Words and Music by
TIM WHEELER

G
C
and set - tle in as the wea - ther folds in the slow haze of the
B5
G
af - ter - noon. Sway - ing hips, made like a gun,
C
B5
Am
black - est sails. The most beau - ti - ful star in the world
D
A
in the air, on my tongue, be - fore my eyes, be -

D
yond the stars, be - neath the sun. So
G
Em
Cadd9
take me in your arms a - gain,
D
G
Em
Cadd9
lead me in my dreams a - gain.
D
G
A
Cadd9
So what is it worth?

D G A Cadd9

To Coda ⊕

I'd sell my soul, what is it worth?

1.

D B5

Only you know.

2.

D

Only you know.

Em

Play 3 times

ad lib.

Verse 2:
You were conceived in my heart
Came like a dream
To save me from my mortality
Put on your dress
And settle in as the weather folds
Our lives will be entwined
Even when I die
You'll see me through 'til the end of time
No earthly bride.

LOVE WILL COME THROUGH

from MOONLIGHT MILE

Words and Music by
FRAN HEALY

Bm G D F#7 Bm G
— it and keep it a - live? 'Cause it's burn - ing a hole and I can't
— got a feel - ing it's right. If it's real, what I'm feel - ing is no
D F#7 Bm G D F#7
— get to sleep and I can't live a - lone in this lie. So look up,
— make - be - lieve in the sound of the waves of the flight of a dove.
Bm G D F#7 Bm G
take it a - way. Don't look da da da down this moun -
D F#7 Bm G D F#7
- tain. If the world is - n't turn - ing your heart won't re - turn a - ny - one,

Bm
G
D
F#7
Bm
G
— a - ny - thing, a - ny - how. ——— So take — me, don't
D
F#7/C#
Bm
G
D
F#7/C#
leave me. Take me don't leave me.
Bm
G
D
F#7/A#
Bm
G
To Coda
Ba - by, love will come through, it's just wait - ing for you.
1
D
F#7/C#
2. As I stand
2
D
F#7/C#
Bm
G

D
F♯7/C♯
Bm
G
D
F♯7/C♯
Bm
G
D
F♯7/A♯
Bm
G
D
F♯7/C♯
All will come.
Bm
Take it a - way, don't look da da da down.
If the world
Bm
G
D
F♯7
is - n't turn - ing your heart won't re - turn a - ny - one,

Bm
G
D
F♯7
D.S. al Coda
— a - ny - thing, a - ny - how. So take
Coda
D
F♯7/C♯
Bm
G
D
F♯7/C♯
Love will come through, yeah.
Bm
G
D
F♯7/C♯
Bm
G
Love will come through.
D
F♯7/A♯
Bm
G
D
F♯7/C♯
Bm
Love will come through.

A LOVE BEFORE TIME

from the Motion Picture CROUCHING TIGER, HIDDEN DRAGON

Words and Music by JAMES SCHAMUS,
TAN DUN and JORGE CALANDRELLI

Gm11
3 fr
Gm/F
Em11
7 fr
A7sus
Am7
moun - tains dis - ap - peared, if the
Dm7
Dm/C
B♭maj13
seas ran dry, turned to dust, and the
If the years take a - way ev - 'ry
Dm
Am7
B♭maj9
C7sus
sun re - fused to rise, I would
mem - 'ry that I have, I would
F
C/E
B♭6
still find my way by the
still know the way that would

Dm
C6
light I see in your eyes. The world I
lead me back to your side. The North
B♭sus2
6fr
B♭
To Coda
C
know fades away, (As the earth
Star may but you
Dm9
Dm/C
B♭maj7
reclaims its due and the cycle starts anew,
stay.
F/A
Gm11
3fr
B♭maj7
we'll stay, always), in the love that we have shared

A7sus
Am7
Dsus
be - fore time.
D.S. al Coda
CODA
C
F
die, but the light that I
C/E
B♭6
Dsus
see in your eyes will burn there

C6
B♭sus2
6fr
B♭
al - ways, lit by the love we have
C
F/A
Dm
(When the for - est turns to jade and the sto -
shared be - fore time.
B♭maj7
F/A
Gm7
- ries that we've made dis - solve a - way), one shin -
A7sus
Am7
Dm
Dm/C
- ing light will still re - main. (When we shed our earth - ly skin and when our real

B♭maj7
F/A
Gm11
3 fr
Gm/F
life be - gins there'll be no shame); just the love
B♭maj7
A7sus
Am7
Dsus
that we have made be - fore time.
Moderately, somewhat freely
Dm
C6
B♭
Dsus2

LOVE IS ALL AROUND

from FOUR WEDDINGS AND A FUNERAL

C
Dm
F
G
C
Dm
writ-ten on the wind, it's ev-'ry-where I go, oh, yes it is.
give your prom-ise to me and I give mine to you.
F
G
C
Dm
F
G
So if you real-ly love me, come on and let it show,
I need some-one be-side me in ev-'ry-thing I do,
C
Dm
F
G
N.C.
oh.
oh, yes I do.
F
Dm
F
You know I love you, I al-ways will.
My mind's made up by the

C
F
Dm
way that I feel. _ There's no be - gin - ning, there'll be no _ end, _ 'cause
1
G
on my _ love _ you can de - pend. _
C
Dm
F
Gsus
C
Dm
F
Gsus
2
G
Gsus
G
Gsus
I can de - pend. _

G
Gsus
G
C
Dm
Got-ta keep it mov - ing.
Ooh, it's writ-ten in the wind, oh,
F
G
C
Dm
F
G
ev-'ry-where I go.
So
C
Dm
F
G
C
Dm
if you real - ly love me, love me, love me,
come on and let it show.
F
G
C
Dm
F
G
Repeat and Fade
Come on and let it show.
Come on and let it show.

LOVEFOOL

from WILLIAM SHAKESPEARE'S ROMEO + JULIET

Music by PETER SVENSSON
Lyrics by NINA PERSSON
and PETER SVENSSON

1,3
2,4
C♯dim7
Dm7
D♯dim7
So I cry and I pray
E5
A6
Bm9
E7
and I beg. (Love me, love me,) say that you love me.
Amaj7
Bm9
E7add13
A6
Bm9
(Fool me, fool me,) go on and fool me. (Love, me, love me,) pre-tend
E7add13
Amaj7
Bm9
E7add13
that you love me. (Leave me, leave me,) just say that you need me.

F#m7
Bm7
2fr
E9
So I cry
and I beg
Amaj7
D
E
A6
Bm9
E7add13
for you to (love me, love me.) Say that you love me.
Amaj7
Bm9
E7add13
A
Dm
To Coda
(Leave me, leave me,) just say that you need me. I can't care a-bout
E+
Am7
D.S. al Coda
an-y-thing but you.

CODA
E+
A
Bm9
E7add13
an - y - thing but you. (An - y - thing but
Amaj7
Bm9
E7add13
A6
Bm9
E7add13
you.) (Love me, love _ me,) say that you love me. _
Amaj7
Bm9
E7add13
A6
Bm9
(Fool me, fool _ me,) go on and fool me. (Love me, love _ me.)
E7add13
A
Dm
E+
Am
I know that you need me. I can't care a-bout an - y - thing but you.
molto rit.

LULLABY FOR CAIN

from Paramount Pictures' and Miramax Films' THE TALENTED MR. RIPLEY

Lyrics by ANTHONY MINGHELLA
Music by GABRIEL YARED

be - lov - ed sons of mine.
mf
Sing a lull - a - bye,
mf
mother - er is close
mf
by.
In - no - cent eyes, such in - no - cent
eyes.
sub. mp
En - vy stole your broth - er's life,
sub. mp

mf
came home, mur - dered peace of mind.
mf
Left you night - mares on the pil - low, __
mp
__ sleep now. __
mp
mf
Soul, sur-ren - der-ing your soul the heart of you not
mf
whole for __ love, ______ but __ love ______ what _

f
mf
toll? Cast in - to the dark, brand - ed with the mark
mf
of shame of Cain.
mp
From the gar - den of God's light
mp
3
mf
to a wil - der - ness of night.
mp
Sleep now, sleep now.
mf
mf

MOST OF THE TIME

from HIGH FIDELITY

Words and Music by
BOB DYLAN

C
F
Am
G
ev - er I stum-ble up - on.
I don't ev - en no - tice she's
F
To Coda
C
F
C
gone, Most of the time.
1, 2.
3.
F
F
G
Am
G
2,3. Most of the time
Most of the time
C
G
Am
G
C
she ain't ev-en in my mind,
I would-n't know her if I saw her,
She's that far be - hind.

Verse 2:
Most of the time
It's well understood
Most of the time
I wouldn't change it if I could
I can make it all match up,
I can hold my own,
I can deal with the situation
Right down to the bone.
I can survive,
I can endure,
And I don't even think, about her,
Most of the time.

Verse 3:
Most of the time
My head is on straight,
Most of the time
I'm strong enough to hate.
I don't build up illusion
'Til it makes me sick,
I ain't afraid of confusion
No matter how thick.
I can smile in the face.
Of mankind.
Don't even remember
What her lips felt like on mine
Most of the time.

Verse 4:
Most of the time
I'm halfway content,
Most of the time
I know exactly where it all went,
I don't cheat on myself,
I don't run and hide,
Hide from the feelings
That are buried inside,
I don't compromise
And I don't pretend.
I don't even care
If I ever see her again
Most of the time.

A NEW WORLD

from SHAKESPEARE IN LOVE

Composed by
STEPHEN WARBECK

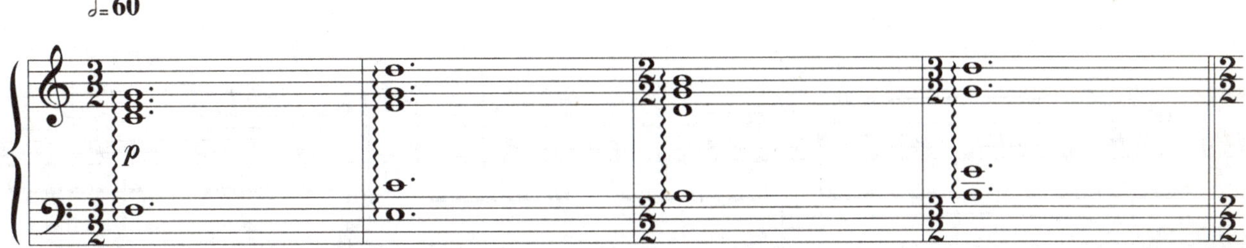

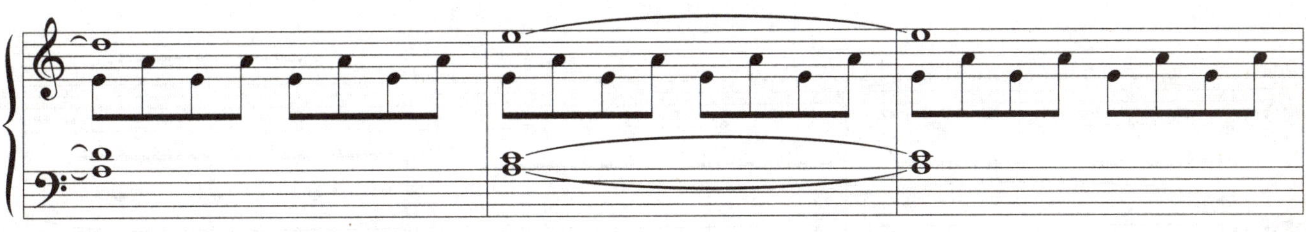

mp
cresc.

mf
dim.

mp
cresc.
mf cresc.

f dim.
mp

OH, PRETTY WOMAN

from PRETTY WOMAN

Words and Music by ROY ORBISON
and BILL DEES

D
E7
wom - an
I don't be - lieve you, you're not the
wom - an
that you look love - ly as can
truth
No one could look as good as
be
Are you lone - ly just like
N.C.
you.
me?
Mer - cy.
1
E7
2
E7
Pret - ty

Dm
G7
Pret - ty wom - an stop a - while, ___
C
Am
Dm
Pret - ty wom - an talk a - while, _
Pret - ty wom - an
G7
C
give your smile _ to me.
Dm
G7
C
Pret - ty wom - an yeah, yeah, yeah, ________
Pret - ty wom - an

Am
Dm
look my way,
Pret - ty wom - an
G7
C
A7
say you'll stay with me.
'Cause I
F♯m
Dm
E7
need you
I'll treat you right.
A
F♯m
Dm
Come with me ba - by.
Be mine to -

E7
night.
A
F♯m
Pret - ty wom - an don't walk on by, Pret - ty
A
F♯m
wom - an don't make me cry, Pret - ty
D
E7
wom - an don't walk a - way.

Hey,
O. K.
If that's the way it must be
O. K.
I guess I'll go on home, it's late
There'll be to -
mor - row night but wait!
N.C.
What do I see?

E7
Is she walk - ing back to -
me?
Yeah, she's
walk - ing back to me!
A
Oh, Pret - ty wom - an.

ON GOLDEN POND

Main Theme from ON GOLDEN POND

Music by DAVE GRUSIN

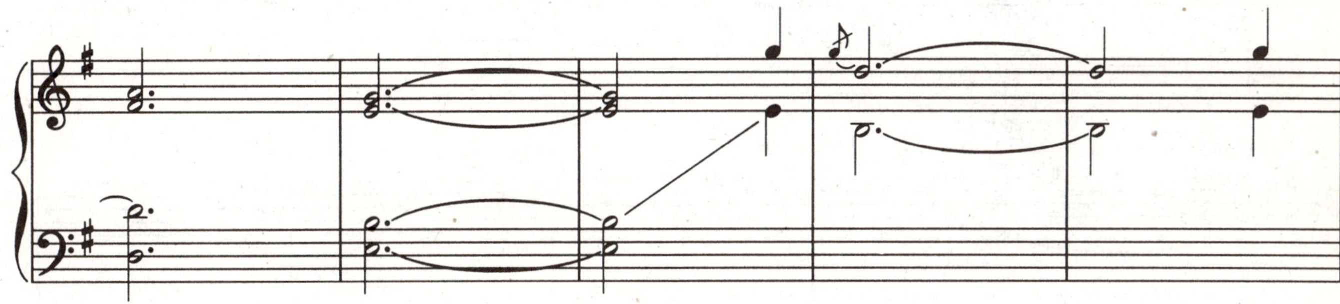

*Not fast and somewhat freely

Am
E7(no 3rd)/A
Am
C/D
D
C/D
G
Ped.
8va
L.H.
R.H.
Em
D/F♯
G7/4
G7
Cadd9
G/B
Am7
Ped.
D
D7/4
G
8va
Ped.
G
G/B
C
8va
poco animato
Ped.
Ped.

8va
Am
D
G
D7
G
D7
G
D/F♯
Em
Ped.
Am7
G/B
Cmaj7
C6
Ped.
D4
D
G
gliss.
Am
L.H.
quasi harp
Ped.
D
Am
Em

C
G
A
Eadd2(no 3rd)
Ped.
8va
*
D
Am
Dm
Am
C
F
C/E
C
D4
L.H.
Ped.
G pedal
*
8va

Cmaj7
G/B
Am
Ped.
*
D7/4
Em
Ped.
Am7
*
G/B
Cmaj7
C6
D4
D
G
Ped. al fine
ppp

ONE DAY I'LL FLY AWAY

from the Motion Picture MOULIN ROUGE

Words and Music by WILL JENNINGS
and JOE SAMPLE

Bm
Bm7/A
Em7
A
Gm/D
D
What more could your love do for me? When will love be through with me?
Bm
Em9
A
A♯dim
Bm
Why live life from dream to dream, and _ dread the day when _
G
F♯
Em7
Bm7/F♯
dream - ing ends? ___
With growing intensity
Em7
D/F♯
Gm
3 fr
Dm

Gm
3 fr
A
Asus
A
molto rall.
D
Gm6/D
D
Bm
Em7
A
One day I'll fly a - way, leave all this to yes - ter - day.
a tempo
Dm
Dm7
Gm9
3 fr
C
C♯dim7
Dm
B♭
A
Why live life from dream to dream, and dread the day when dream - ing
Dm
B
Em6/C♯
B
Em6/B
B
ends? One day I'll fly a - way, fly, fly, a - way.

READY TO TAKE A CHANCE AGAIN
(Love Theme)
from the Paramount Picture FOUL PLAY

Words by NORMAN GIMBEL
Music by CHARLES FOX

F/G
G9
F/G
G9
C
G/B
No jolts, no sur - pris - es,
Gm/B♭
A7sus
A7
no cri - sis a - ris - es. My life goes a - long
Dm
Dm/C
as it should, it's all ver - y nice, but

Dm/B
Dm/E
E7♭9
Am7
not ver - y good. And I'm read - y to take a chance
rall.
a tempo
Dm7
F/G
G/F
C/E
Am/E
E7/G♯
a - gain, read - y to put my love on the line with
Am
Am/G
G♭7♭5
Fmaj7
Em7
Dm7
Em7
you. Been liv - ing with noth - ing to show for it. You
Dm7
F/G
G/F
C/E
Fmaj7
To Coda
get what you get when you go for it, and I'm read - y to take a chance

E/G♯
a - gain with you.
Am
E/G♯
A/G
When she left me in all my de - spair,
A7
Dm
Dm/C
I just held on. My hopes were all gone, then
D.S. al Coda
Dm/B
Dm/E
E7♭9
C/E
Fmaj7
CODA
I found you there. And I'm
read - y to take a chance

F♯m7♭5
4fr
C/G
E/G♯
a - gain,
read - y to take a chance a - gain with you,
Am7
with
you.
Dm7
F/G
G/F
C/E
Am/E
E7/G♯
Repeat ad lib. and Fade
Am7
Dm7
F/G
G/F
C/E
Am/E
E7/G♯

PART OF YOUR WORLD

from Walt Disney's THE LITTLE MERMAID

Lyrics by HOWARD ASHMAN
Music by ALAN MENKEN

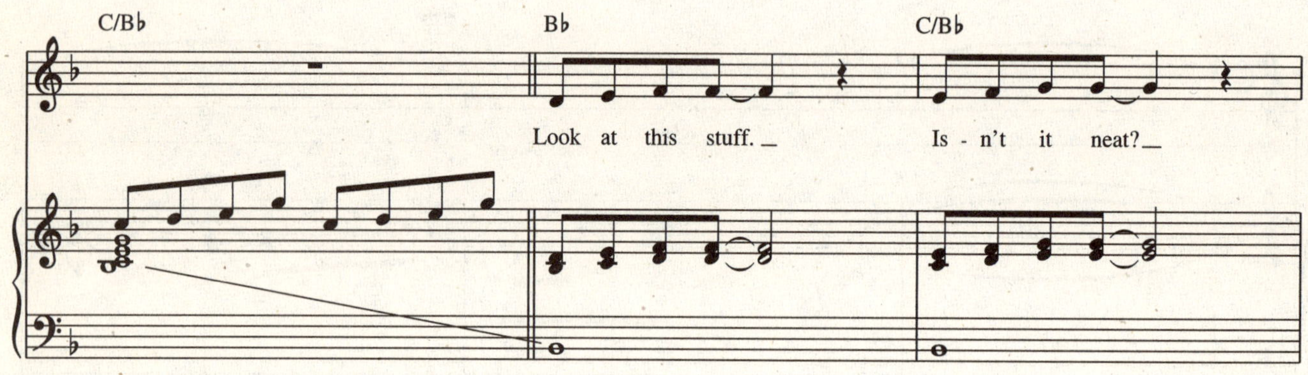

B♭
C/B♭
B♭
Look at this trove, _ treas - ures un - told. _ How man - y won - ders can
C/B♭
Am7
Dm7
one ca - vern hold? Look - ing a - round _ here you'd think, _ sure, she's got
F/G
G7
B♭maj7
ev - 'ry - thing. _ I've got gad - gets and giz - mos a -
Am7
F/A
Dm7
F/G
G7
plen - ty. I've got who - zits and what - zits ga - lore. You want

B♭maj7
Am7
F/A
rall.
Dm7
thing - a - ma-bobs, I've got twen - ty. But who cares? No big
F/G
G7
B♭/C
a tempo
Am/C
B♭/C
C7
deal. I want more.
F
Am7
B♭
I wan - na be where the peo - ple are. I wan - na see wan - na
B♭/C
C
Dm
Am
see 'em danc - in', walk - in' a - round on those, what - d - ya call 'em, oh

Bb/C
C
C7
F
feet.
Flip - pin' your fins ___ you don't
F/A
Bb
Bb/C
C
get too far. ___
Legs are re - quired ___ for jump - in', danc - in'.
Dm
Am
F/A
Bb/C
Stroll - in' a - long ___ down the, what's that word a - gain, street.
C7
F
F/Eb
Up where they walk, up where they run, up where they

B♭/D
B♭m/D♭
F/C
stay all day in the sun. Wan - der - in' free, wish I could
B♭/C
C
F
be part of that world. What would I
B♭
C/B♭
Am
give if I could live out - ta these wa - ters.
Dm
B♭
C/B♭
What would I pay to spend a day warm on the

Am
F7sus
F7
B♭
sand.
Bet - cha on land they un - der -
C/B♭
A7sus
A7
Dm
Dm/C
stand. Bet they don't re - pri - mand their daugh - ters. Bright young
F/G
G
F/G
G
E♭maj7
rall.
a tempo
wom - en, sick of swim - min' read - y to stand.
B♭/C
C
B♭/C
C
F
F/A
And read - y to know what the peo - ple know.

B♭maj7
B♭/C
C7
Ask 'em my ques - tions and get some an - swers.
Dm
Am
F/A
What's a fire, and why does it, what's the word,
Gm7
C7
F
burn. When's it my turn? Would - n't I
3
F/E♭
B♭/D
B♭m/D♭
love, love to ex - plore that shore up a - bove,
3

slower
F
out of the sea.
Wish I could
slower
B♭/C
C7
B♭
be
part of that world.
L.H.
C/B♭
B♭
C/B♭
F

PICNIC

from the Columbia Technicolor Picture PICNIC

Words by STEVE ALLEN
Music by GEORGE W. DUNING

C Dm7 G9 C Dm7 G7+ C
You and I in the sun-shine We strolled the fields and farms At the
3
Am Am7 Am6 D7 Dm7 G7 sus.4 C F G9
last light of eve-ning I held you in my arms Now when days grow
C Dm6 Am7 Am6 D7 Dm7 G7sus. G7 Dm7 G7-9
stor-my And lone-ly for me I just re-call Pic-nic time with
1. C Cdim G7sus.4 G7
you. On a
2. C Dm9 Db7 C
you.
L.H.

PSYCHO
(Prelude)
Theme from the Paramount Picture PSYCHO

Music by
BERNARD HERRMANN

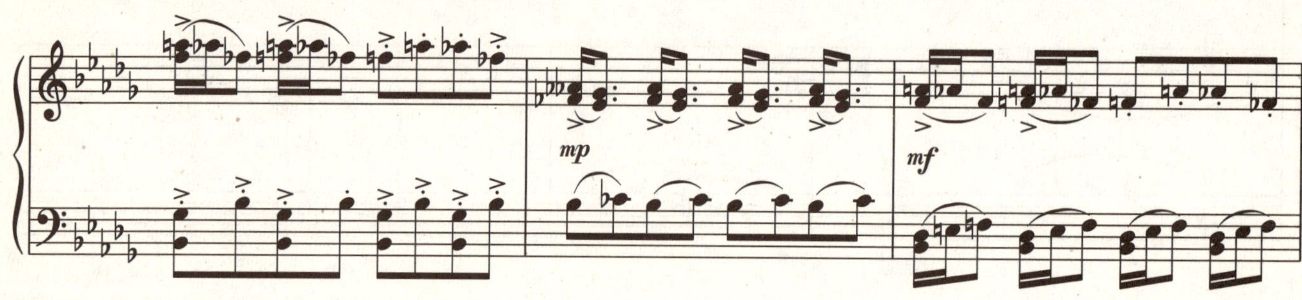

sfz mp
f
f
sfz mp

f
mp
f
dim.
f

f
dim.
mf
f
f
sffz

RAIDERS MARCH

from the Paramount Motion Picture RAIDERS OF THE LOST ARK

Music by JOHN WILLIAMS

March tempo

B♭/C
C
3
B♭/C

A♭/C
3
G/C
cresc.
F/C

B♭/C
mf
Am7
3
B♭/C

A♭/C
3
C
B♭/C
Am7
3

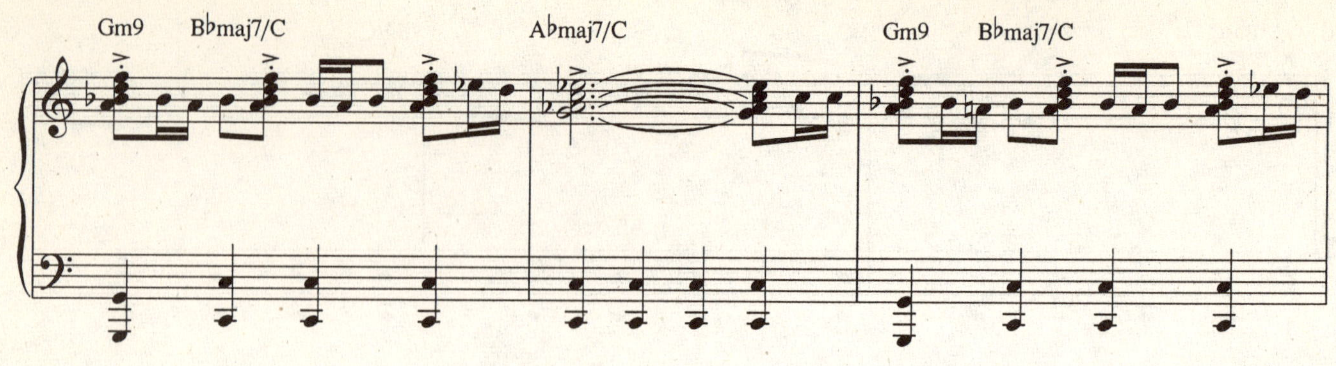
Gm9
B♭maj7/C
A♭maj7/C
Gm9
B♭maj7/C

A♭maj7/C
Gm9
Fm9

Cmaj7
f
C

F/C
G7/C
C
sim.

D♭
G7sus
1
2
Csus
C/F
C
mf
Gm9
Cmaj7
Gm9
Cmaj7
f
A♭maj7/G
Gm9
Cmaj7
ff
8vb

ROMEO AND JULIET

(Love Theme)

from the Paramount Picture ROMEO AND JULIET

By NINO ROTA

mf
mp

mf
cresc.
f
mf
1.
2.
mp
rit.
mf
a tempo
mp
rit.

SOMETHING GOOD
from THE SOUND OF MUSIC

Lyrics and Music by
RICHARD RODGERS

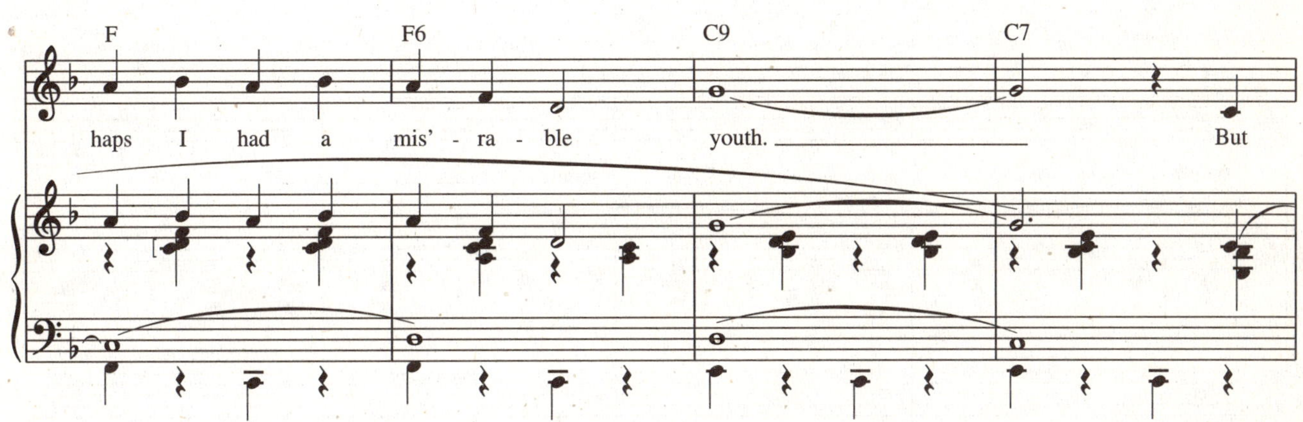

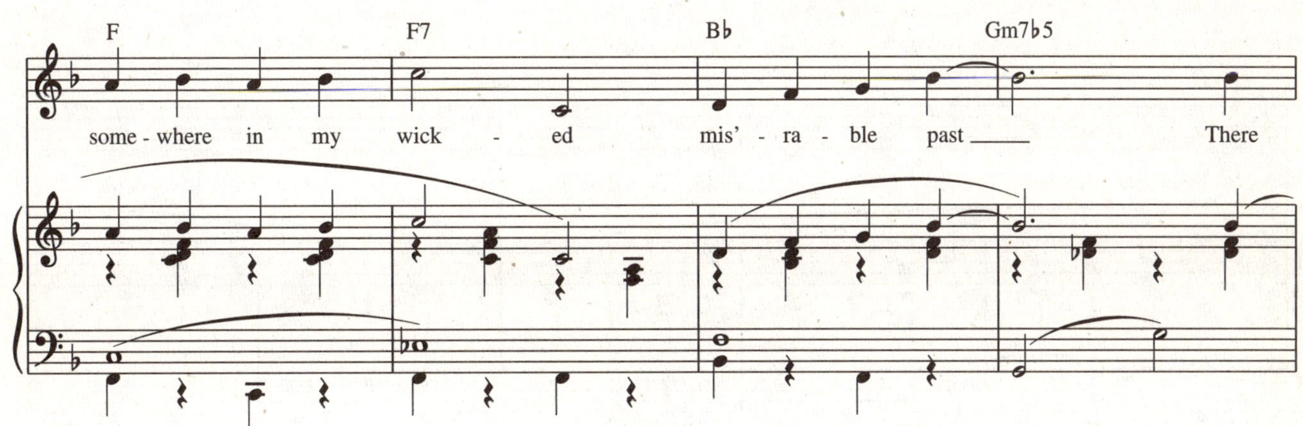

F/C
C7
F6
F7
must have been a mo - ment of truth.
For
Bb/D
Db7
F/C
F
here you are, Stand - ing there, Lov - ing me,
mf
Bb/D
Db7
C9
C7
Wheth - er or not you should.
So,
mp
F
F7
Bb
Gm7b5
F/C
some-where in my youth or child - hood
I must have done

1.
2.
E/C C7 F Gm7/C C7 F
some - thing good. Per - good.
mf
Coda
C7/B♭ Am7 F/A Gm7 Gm7♭5
Noth - ing comes from noth - ing, Noth - ing ev - er could. So,
F/C B♭/C C7
some - where in my youth or child - hood I
F/C E/C C7 F
must have done some - thing good.

SEIZE THE DAY

from Walt Disney's NEWSIES

Lyrics by JACK FELDMAN
Music by ALAN MENKEN

Hymn-like

C G7 C

mf

David: O - pen the gates and seize the day.

Dm C

Don't be a - fraid and don't de - lay.

B♭ F C G/B Am

Noth - ing can break us. No one can

Fm6/A♭
C/G
G7
G♯dim7
Am
D7/F♯
make us give our rights a - way. A -
C/G
G7sus
G7
Brightly
C
rise and seize the day.
rit.
David: Now is the time to seize the day.

B♭ F

Newsies: (Now is the time to seize the day.) *David:* Send out the call and join the fray.

C Dm/C C

Newsies: (Send out the call and join the fray.) *David:* Wrongs will __ be right - ed

Am G F G7 C

if we're _ u - nit - ed. *All:* Let us __ seize _ the day.

C

Friends of the friend - less seize the day.

B♭
F
(Friends of the friend - less, seize the day.) Raise up the torch and light the way.
C
Dm/C
C
Am
G
F
(Raise up the torch and light the way.) Proud and _ de - fi - ant we'll slay _ the gi - ant.
F
G7
C
Let us ___ seize ___ the day. ___
Am
C7/G
F
F
G
___ Neigh-bor to neigh - bor, ___ fa - ther to

Asus
A/C♯
Dm
C/E
son,
one
for
F
G
C
all
and
all
for
one.
C
O - pen the gates and seize the day.
(O - pen the gates and seize the day.)
Don't be a - fraid and don't de - lay.
B♭
F

C
Dm/C
C
Am
G
F
(Don't be a-fraid and don't de-lay.) Noth - ing _ can break us. No one _ can make us
G7
C
Am
C7/G
give our rights _ a - way. Neigh-bor to
F
G
Asus
neigh - bor, fa - ther to son
A/C#
Dm
C/E
F
G
C
one for all and all _ for one.

SHE
from NOTTING HILL

Lyric by HERBERT KRETZMER
Music by CHARLES AZNAVOUR

2
D G C Ab
seem in - side her shell
She who al - ways seems so hap - py in a
Eb Db C
crowd whose eyes can be so pri - vate and so proud no - one's al - lowed to see them when they cry
Fm Bb Eb Cm D D7
She may be the love that can - not hope to last may come to me from sha - dows of the past that I re - mem - ber till the
G G7 D.S. al Coda
CODA D G F
day I die.
be the mean - ing of my life is she
C Dm G C
she mm she.
Rit.

SON OF A PREACHER MAN

from PULP FICTION

Words and Music by JOHN HURLEY
and RONNIE WILKINS

C
Lord knows, to my sur - prise, The on - ly one who could ev - er reach me
F
C
was the son - of - a preach - er man; The on - ly boy who could ev - er teach me
F
C
G7
F
was the son - of - a preach - er man, yes he was, he was. Ooh.
1. C
2. Bb
Bb
F
How well I re - mem - ber the look that was in his eyes, Steal - in' kiss - es from me

G7
on the sly, Tak-in' time to make time, Tell-in' me that he's all mine.
C7
Learn-in' from each oth-ers knowin' and look-in' to see how much we've grown, And the
CHORUS
F
Bb
F
on-ly one who could ev-er reach me was the son-of-a preach-er man; The on-ly one who could
f
Repeat Chorus and fade out
Bb
F
C7
Bb
ev-er teach me was the son-of-a preach-er man; Yes he was. Yeah! The

SON OF MAN

from Walt Disney Pictures' TARZAN™

Words and Music by
PHIL COLLINS

G(add2)
all these things will come to you in time.
A
G
On this jour - ney that you're mak -
no one there to guide
D
A
- ing there'll be an - swers that you'll seek,
you, no one to take your hand.
Bm
Bm/A
G
and it's you who'll climb the moun -
But with faith and un - der - stand -

D
A
-tain, it's you who'll reach the peak.
-ing you will jour - ney from boy to man.
Bm
A
G
Son of man, look to
D
A
G
D
A
the sky. Lift your spir - it, set it free.
G
D
A
G
Some-day you'll walk tall with pride. Son of man, a man

1
D
A
D
in time you'll be.
Bm7
2 fr
G(add2)
A
Though there's
2
D
A
E
in time you'll be.

A/E
F#m7/E
D/E
In
E
C#m7
4fr
learn-ing you will teach, and in teach-ing you will learn.
A(add2)
You'll find your place be - side the ones you love.
B(add4)
A/E
Oh, and all the things you've dreamed
3
3

E
B
C♯m
4fr
B
of, the vi - sions that you saw. Well, the
A/E
E
B
time is draw - ing near now; it's yours to claim it all.
C♯m
4fr
B
A
E
B(add4)
Son of man, look to the sky.
A
E
B(add4)
A
Lift your spir - it, set it free. Some-day you'll walk tall

E
B(add4)
A
E
B(add4)
with pride.
Son of man, a man in time you'll
E
C♯m7
4fr
be.
Ee - yeah,
A(add2)
ee - yeah,
ee - yeah.
Son of man,
B(add4)
E
son of man's a man for all to see.

SPEAK SOFTLY, LOVE

(Love Theme)

from the Paramount Picture THE GODFATHER

Words by LARRY KUSIK
Music by NINO ROTA

Bb7/D
Bb7
Eb
3fr
Db/F
Fm6/Ab
6fr
days warmed by the sun, deep vel-vet nights when we are
G
no chord
Cm
Fm/C
one. Speak soft-ly, love, so no one hears us but the sky. The vows of
Fm/C
Cm
Fm6/C
Cm
Fm/C
Fm
love we make will live un-til we die. My life is yours and all be-
Cm
Cm/G
G7sus
G7
1
2
cause you came in-to my world with love so soft-ly, love. Speak soft-ly, love.
rit.

STEP BY STEP

from the Touchstone Motion Picture THE PREACHER'S WIFE

Words and Music by
ANNIE LENNOX

D7sus
G
'Cause I'm tak - ing it
step by step,
D/F#
bit by bit,
Em7
Bm7
2fr
stone by stone,
yeah,
brick by brick.
Gmaj7/B
C
Oh, yeah.
Step by step,

Bm7
2fr
Em7
C
day by day,
mile by mile,
ooh.
G/D
And this old
G
road is rough in ru - in,
so man-y dan - gers a - long the way.
So man-y bur - dens might fall up - on me,
so man-y trou -

Bm7
2 fr
G/B
C
-bles that I have to face. Oh, but I won't let my spir-it fail
Bm7/E
Em
me. Mm, I won't let my spir-it go un - til I get
C
Em7
to my des-ti-na - tion. I'm gon-na take it slow
D7sus
G
be-cause I'm mak-ing it up step by step. You know I'm tak -

D/F#
Em7
ing it bit by bit, bit by bit, come on, stone by stone,
Bm7
2fr
Gmaj7/B
yeah, brick by brick.
Brick by brick by brick by brick.
C
Cmaj7
Bm7/E
Mm. Step by step, step by step, oh, day by day,
Cmaj7
mile by mile, ooh.

Em7
D7sus
To Coda
G
Go your own way,
go your own way.
Don't give up.
D/F♯
You've got to hold on to what you've got.
Oh, ba -
Em7
Bm7
2 fr
by, don't give up.
You've got to keep on mov - in', don't
Cmaj7
stop. Yeah, yeah.
I know you're hurt - ing,

Em9
Cmaj7
and I know you're blue.
I know you're hurt-
Em7
D7sus
- ing,
but don't let the bad things get to you.
N.C.
G
D.S. al Coda
CODA
G
I'm tak-ing it step by step.
Come on, babe, got to keep mov-ing.
D/F#
Come on, babe, got to keep mov-ing. Come on, babe, got to keep mov-in'. Come on, babe, got to keep mov-in'.
(Bit by bit.)

Em7
Bm7
2fr
Come on, babe, got _ to keep mov-in'. Come on, babe, got _ to keep mov-in.' Come on, babe, got _ to keep mov-in.'
(Stone by stone.) _ (Yeah.) _ (Brick by brick.)
Cmaj7
Come on, ba - by. Come on, babe, got _ to keep mov-in'. Come on, babe, got _ to keep mov-in'.
(Step by step.)
Bm7/E
Em
Cmaj7
Come on, babe, got _ to keep mov-in'. Come on, babe, got _ to keep mov - in'. Come on, babe, got _ to keep mov-in'.
(Day by day.) (Mile by mile.) _
Bm7/E
D7sus
Repeat and Fade
Come on, babe, got _ to keep mov-in'. Come on, babe, got _ to keep mov-in'. Come on, babe, got _ to keep mov-in'.
(Go your own way.) (Go your own way.)

THEME FROM "TERMS OF ENDEARMENT"

from the Paramount Picture TERMS OF ENDEARMENT

By MICHAEL GORE

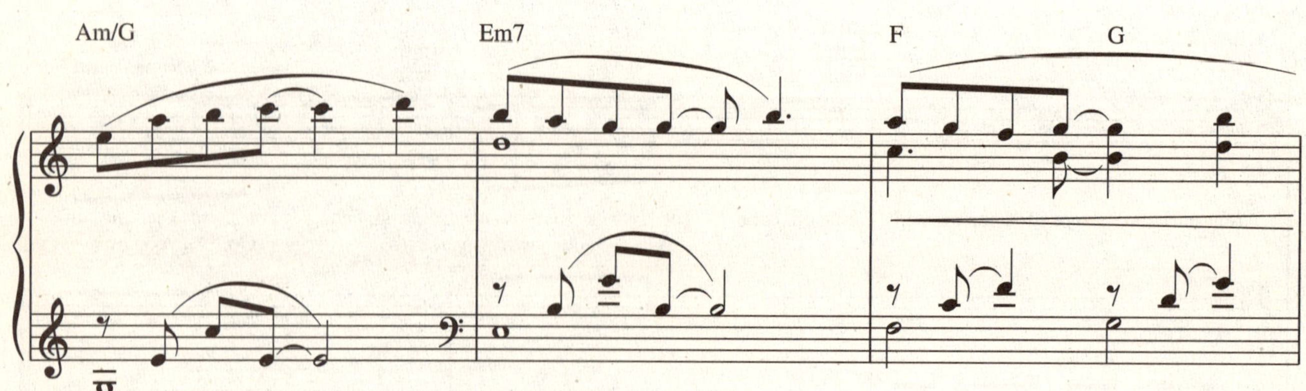

C
Csus
C
mf

Csus
C
F/C
C
mp

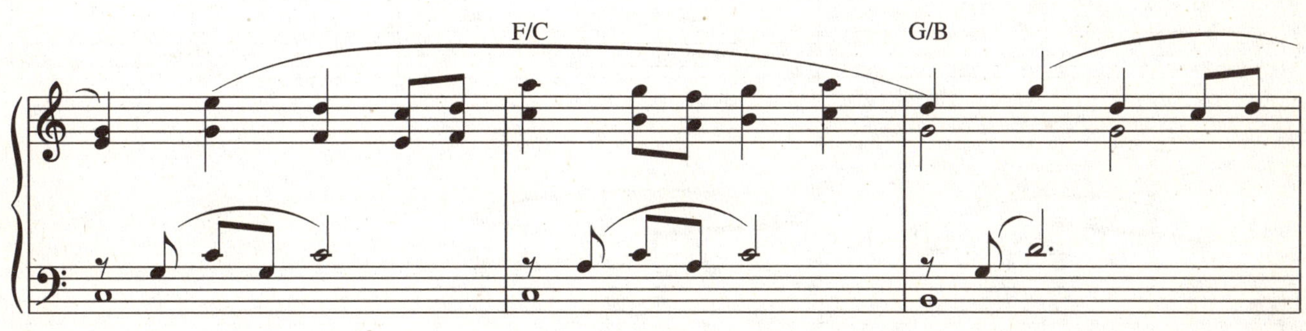
F/C
G/B

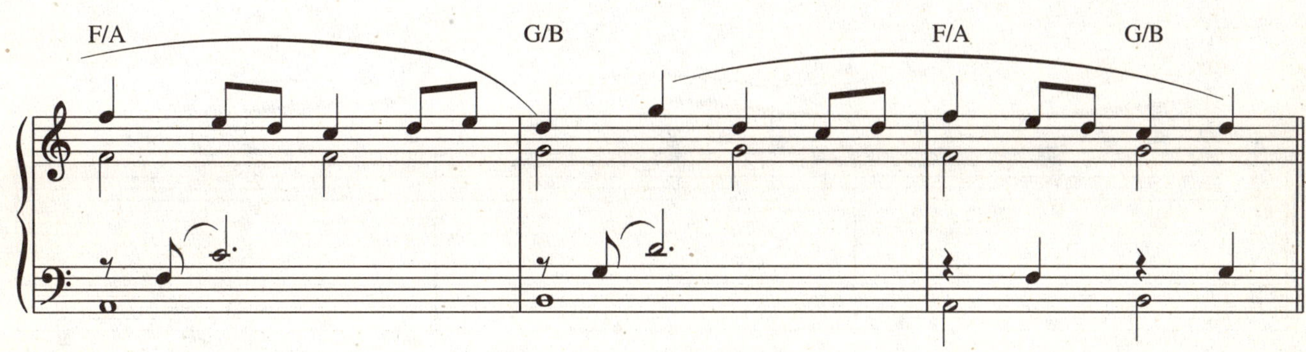
F/A
G/B
F/A
G/B

C
F/C
C
(mp)
F/C
G/B
F/A
G/B
F/A
G/B
Am
f
Em7
Am
Am/G
Em7

F
G
ff
C
p
F/C
sim.
C
F/C
G/C
C
G/C
F/C
C
Am
mf
Em
sim.

Fmaj7
F
G
C/E
mp
mf
F
Gsus
G
F
G
mp
F
G
Am
f
Em7
Am
Am/G
Em7
F
G

C
Csus
C
mf
Csus
C
Csus
C
mp
F/C
C
F/C
C
F/C
C
F/G
C
rit. e dim.
p

THIS YEAR'S LOVE

from THIS YEAR'S LOVE

Words and Music by
DAVID GRAY

D♭add9
E♭
fr3
A♭
fr4
Fm
time. I've been wait - ing on my own too long.
D♭add9
E♭
D♭add9
E♭
And when you hold me like you do it feels so right, oh now,
D♭add9
E♭
A♭
I start to for - get how my heart gets torn when that
(Verse 3 see block lyric)
Fm
1. B♭7
D♭
hurt gets thrown; feel - ing like I can't go on.

2, 3.

B♭7 D♭ A♭

dream in - side my soul, when you kiss me on that mid - night street, sweep me

Fm B♭7 D♭ *To Coda* ⊕

off my feet, sing - ing ain't this life so sweet?

D♭add9 E♭ D♭add9 E♭ D♭add9 E♭

This year's love had bet - ter last.

A♭ Fm D♭add9 E♭ D♭add9 E♭ **D.𝄋. al Coda** *(As 2°)*

This year's love had bet - ter last.

Verse 2:
Turning circles and time again
It cuts like a knife, oh now
If you love me I got to know for sure
'Cause it takes something more this time
Than sweet, sweet lies, oh now
Before I open up my arms and fall
Losing all control
Every dream inside my soul
When you kiss me on that midnight street
Sweep me off my feet
Singing ain't this life so sweet.

Verse 3:
'Cause who's to worry if our hearts get torn
When that hurt gets thrown?
Don't you know this life goes on?
Won't you kiss me on that midnight street
Sweep me off my feet
Singing ain't this life so sweet?

A TOUCH OF EVIL

from A TOUCH OF EVIL

By HENRY MANCINI

3
Bb
Fm
Bb
Fm
Bb
Fm

B♭
Fm
B♭
Fm
B♭
Fm
B♭
N.C.
(Bongos)
poco dim

UNCHAINED MELODY

featured in the Motion Picture GHOST

Lyric by HY ZARET
Music by ALEX NORTH

G
Em
Bm
D
D7
much, are you still mine? I
poco rall.
G
D6/F#
Em7
Gmaj7/D
need your love, I need your love, God
a tempo
Am/C
D7
G
speed your love to me!
poco rall.
a tempo
C
D
C
Lone - ly riv - ers flow to the sea, to the
Lone - ly moun - tains gaze at the stars, at the
R.H.
L.H.
poco accel.

B♭
C
D
sea, to the o - pen arms of the
stars, wait - ing for the dawn of the
R.H.
L.H.
R.H.
L.H.
G
C
sea. Lone - ly riv - ers
day. All a - lone, I
D
C
B♭
sigh, "Wait for me, wait for me!"
gaze at the stars, at the stars,
R.H.
L.H.
R.H.
L.H.
R.H.
L.H.
C
D
G
I'll be com - ing home, wait for me!
dream - ing of my love far a - way.
R.H.
L.H.

Tempo I
G
Em
Cmaj7
Oh, my love, my dar - ling, I've
p
D7
G
Em
hun - gered for your touch a long, lone - ly
D
D7
G
Em
time. Time goes by so
Cmaj7
D7
G
Em
slow - ly and time can do so much, are you still

Bm
D
D7
G
mine?
I need your love,
mf
poco rall.
a tempo
D6/F#
Em7
Gmaj7/D
Am/C
I need your love,
God speed your love
D7
1 G
to me!
poco rall.
a tempo
2 G
Em
Cmaj7
Am7
G(add9)
me!
a tempo
poco rit.

TRUE GRIT

Theme from the Paramount Picture TRUE GRIT

Words by DON BLACK
Music by ELMER BERNSTEIN

F6
Gm7
3fr
C7
Some days, lit - tle girl,
you'll won - der what
Fmaj7
F6
Dm7
Gm7
3fr
life's a - bout,
but oth - ers have known
C7
Fmaj7
F7
few bat - tles are won a - lone.
So, you'll look a -
B♭
B♭maj7
B♭6
B♭
B♭maj7
round to find
some - one who's kind, some -

B♭6
B♭
E♭
E♭maj7
E♭6
E♭
one who is fear - less like you.
The
E♭maj7
E♭6
E♭
E♭maj7
pain of it
will ease a bit when
E♭6
E♭
Gm7
C7
no chord
you find a man with true grit.
One day you will
Gm7
C7
Fmaj7
rise
and you won't be - lieve your eyes.

F6
Dm7
Gm7
3fr
C7
3
__ You'll wake up and see a world that is
Fmaj7
F6
F
Cm7
fine and free. __ Though sum-mer seems far __ a -
F
Fmaj7
way, you will find the sun __ one
day. __

UP WHERE WE BELONG

from the Paramount Picture AN OFFICER AND A GENTLEMAN

Words by WILL JENNINGS
Music by BUFFY SAINTE-MARIE and JACK NITZSCHE

Em7
A
D
D/F♯
road is long. There are moun-tains in our way,
G
G/B
C
A
G/A
A
but we climb a step ev-'ry day.
climb them a
cresc.
D
D/F♯
G
Bm
Love lift us up where we be-long, where the
f
Em
D/F♯
C
G
A
ea-gles cry on a moun-tain high.

D
D/F♯
G
Bm
Love lift us up where we be - long, far from the
Em
D/F♯
1
F♯/A♯
Bm
Gm
3 fr
D
G/D
A/D
world we know; up where we clear winds blow.
3
decresc.
G/D
Gm6/D
2
G/A
A
F
C/E
clear winds blow. Time goes by,
E♭
3 fr
B♭/D
D♭
A♭/C
B♭
Fm7/B♭
E♭
3 fr
no time to cry, life's you and I, a - live, to - day.

Eb
Eb/G
Ab
Cm
3 fr
4 fr
Love lift us up where we be - long, where the
Fm
Eb/G
Db
Ab
Bb
ea - gles cry, on a moun - tain high.
Eb
Eb/G
Ab
Cm
Love lift us up where we be - long far from the
Repeat ad lib. and Fade
Fm
Eb/G
G/B
Cm
Abm
world we know; where the clear winds blow.

WHAT IF I LOVED YOU

from RETURN TO ME

Words and Music by
JOEY GIAN

F#m7
you you're all I've waited for?
A/B
E6
Bm7
E7
And what if I held you tonight and I made
A
D9
4fr
E6
C#m7
you feel oh so right? What if I loved you?
F#m7
A/B
E6
C#m7
F#m7
A/B
Would you always be mine? And what if I kissed

E6
you the way you like to be kissed?
C♯7
What if I held you in my arms so close like this?
F♯m7
A/B
E6
What if I touched you to - night
Bm7
E7
A
D9
4fr
and I filled your bod - y with de - light? What if I loved

E6
C♯7
F♯m7
A/B
E6
you?
Would you al - ways be mine?
F♯m7
B7
E6
E7
A7
3

D7
E6
C#7
F#m7
B7
E6
Oh, what if I sang you a sweet lull - a - by?
And what if I gave you a doz - en stars that I pulled from the sky?
F#m7
A/B
And what if I told

E6
Bm7
E7
A
you to - night
I wan - na love you for the rest of your life?
D9
4fr
E6
C♯m7
F♯m7
A/B
E6
C♯7
What if I loved you?
Would you al - ways be mine?
F♯m7
A/B
E6
C♯7
F♯m7
A/B
E6
E/D
And what if I loved you?
Would you al - ways be mine?
A/C♯
C7
2fr
E/B
N.C.
E7

WHEN THE GOING GETS TOUGH, THE TOUGH GET GOING

from THE JEWEL OF THE NILE

Words and Music by WAYNE BRATHWAITE,
BARRY J. EASTMOND, ROBERT JOHN "MUTT" LANGE
and BILLY OCEAN

N.C.
got something to tell you, I've got something to say,
I'm gon-na put this dream in mo - tion, nev-er let
no - thing stand in my way. (When the go-ing gets tough,)
A
F♯m
E
A
F♯m
E
(the tough get go-ing.)
2. I'm gon-na
3
3
3
3
3

A
F♯m7
E
A
get my - self 'cross the riv - er, that's the price I'm will-ing to pay.
(Verse 3 see block lyric)
D
A
F♯m7
E
I'm gon-na make you stand and de-liv - er, you give me
A
D
E
F♯m
Dadd9
fr2
love in the old - fa-shioned way. Oh. (Dar - ling) I'll climb
E
F♯m
Dadd9
fr2
E
a - ny moun - tain. (Darl - ing) I'll do a - ny - thing. Ooh

A F♯m7 E A F♯m
(ooh,) can I touch you (can I touch you) And do the things that lov-ers do?
E A F♯m E
Ooh, (ooh,) wan-na hold you. (Wan-na hold you) I
A F♯m7 E A F♯m
got-ta get it through to you. Oh, cos when the go-ing gets tough (the
E D
tough get go-ing) When the go-ing gets rough oh, (the tough get rough) Hey

1.
A
F♯m7
E
(hey) hey, hey, hey.
A
F♯m7
E
I'm gon-na
2.
(hey) hey, yeah, yeah. yeah.
A
F♯m7
E
A
D
Saxophone
A
F♯m7
E
A
D

E
F♯m
Dmaj9
fr4
(Dar - ling) I'll climb a - ny moun - tain.
(Dar - ling) I'd swim
ev - 'ry sea.
(Dar - ling) I'd reach for - eign heav - ens
Dadd9
fr2
(Dar - ling) with you lov - ing me.
N.C.
Ooh (ooh) ooh. Can I
Drums

touch you? (Can I touch you?) And do the things that lov-ers do.
(Can I touch you?) Ooh (ooh) wan-na hold you. (Wan-na hold you) I
got-ta get it through to you. Oh, cos when the
A
F♯m
E
D
go-ing gets tough, (go-ing gets tough) (when the go-ing gets rough, oh. (Go-

Verse 3:
I'm gonna buy me a one-way ticket
Nothing's gonna hold me back
Your love's like a soul train coming
And I feel it coming down the track.

(Darling) I'll climb any mountain *etc.*

WISE UP

from MAGNOLIA

Words and Music by
AIMEE MANN

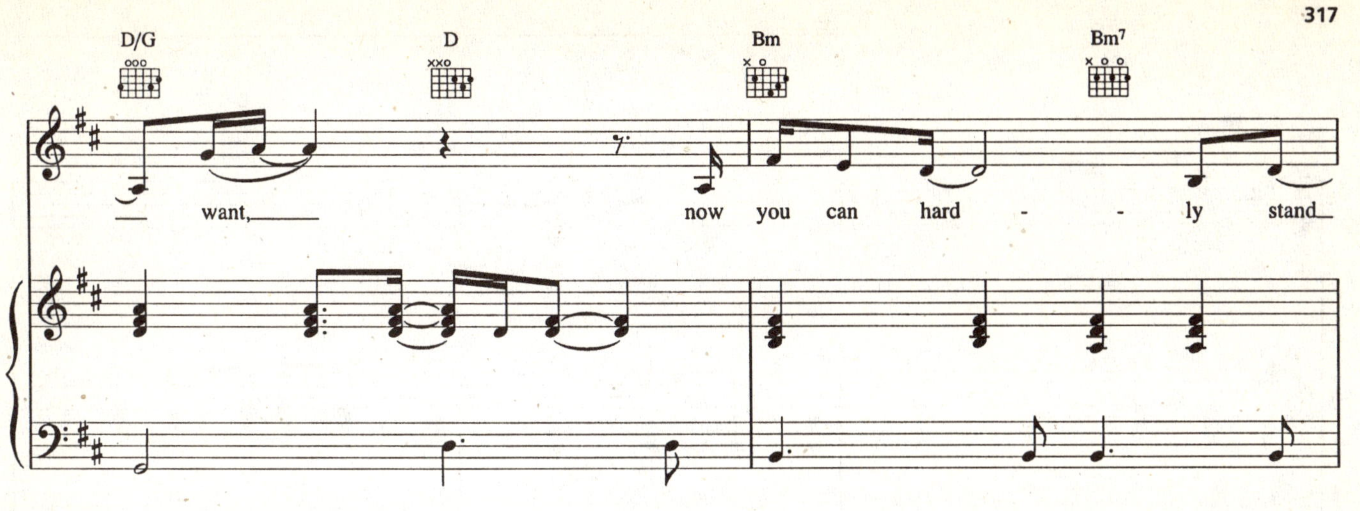
D/G
D
Bm
Bm7
want, now you can hard - - ly stand

G
E
Gadd9
3fr
E
it, though by now you know it's not go - ing to stop,

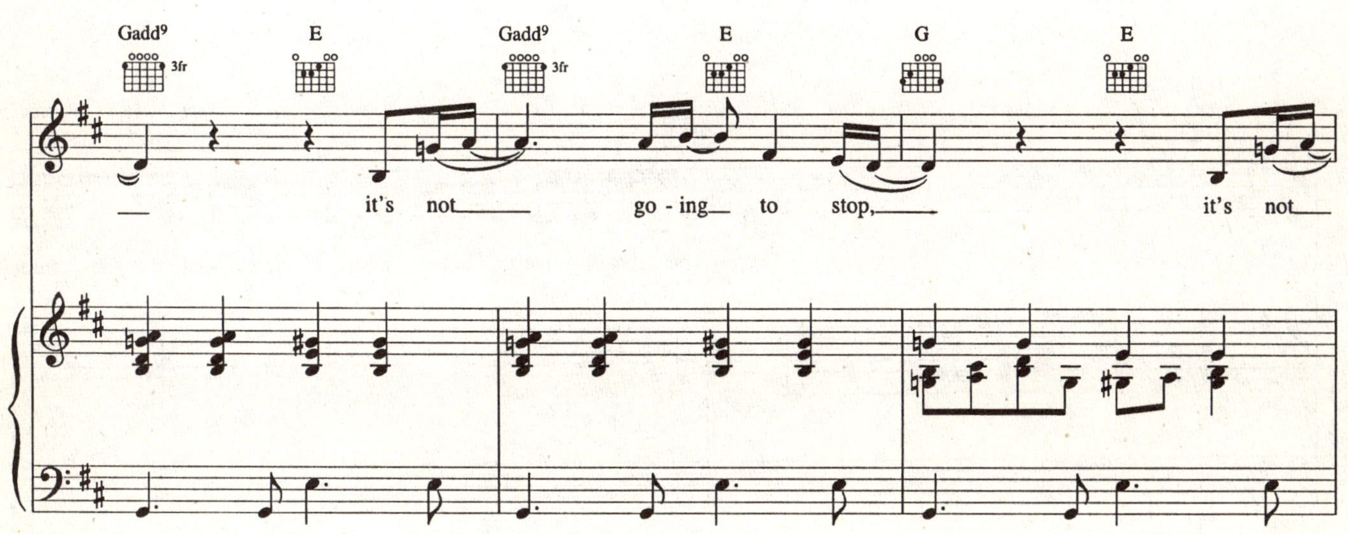
Gadd9
3fr
E
Gadd9
3fr
E
G
E
it's not go - ing to stop, it's not

1.
D
A
C
G
D/G
D
— going to stop till you wise up.
2.
D/G
D
C
G
D/G
D
2. You're — till you wise up.
D/G
D
G
Pre - pare a list for what you need, be - fore

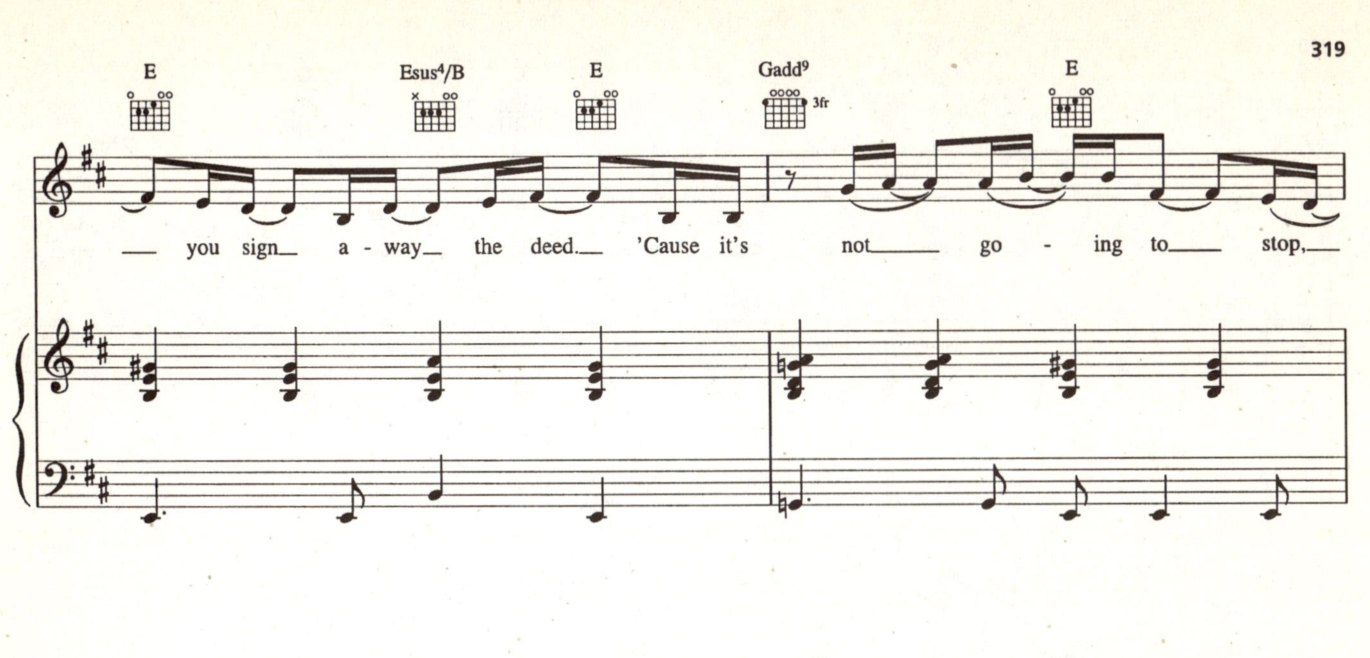
E Esus4/B E Gadd9 E
— you sign — a - way — the deed. — 'Cause it's not — go - ing to — stop, —

Gadd9 E Gadd9 E G E
— it's not — go - ing to — stop, — it's not —

D A C G D A C G
— go - ing to — stop — till you wise up. — No, it's not go - ing to stop — till you wise up. —

Verse 2:
You're sure there's a cure
And you have finally found it.
You think one drink will shrink you till
You're underground and living down.
But it's not going to stop
It's not going to stop
It's not going to stop
Till you wise up.

WOODY'S ROUNDUP

from Walt Disney Pictures' TOY STORY 2 - A Pixar Film

Music and Lyrics by
RANDY NEWMAN

D6
E6
Wood - y's Round - up, come on, it's time to play.
A7
Bm
F♯m
There's Jes - se the yo - del - in' cow - girl. (O - dl
Bm
lay - ee o - dl o ho o - dl lay - ee o - ee.) Bulls - eye, he's
F♯m
Wood - y's horse.
Spoken: He's a smart one.

G
D6
E6
Pete, the old pros - pec - tor, and Wood - y, the man him -
A7
D
Em
Ddim/F
D/F♯
self, of course. It's time for Wood - y's Round - up.
G
G♯dim7
A
A♯dim
Bm
D7/A
He's the ver - y best. He's the root - in' - est toot - in' - est
G
G♯dim
4 fr
D/A
A9
D
cow - boy in the wild, wild West.

D6
B♭6
E7
A
Asus/B
Adim7/C
A7/C#
D6
C#7
Wood - y's
D
G
D
Round - up, come on and gath - er round.

E6
Wood - y's Round - up, where no - bod - y wears a frown.
A7 D Em Ddim/F D/F♯
Bad guys go run - nin'
G G♯dim7 A A♯dim Bm D7/A
when - ev - er he's in town. He's the root - in' - est toot - in' - est
Freely
G G♯dim D/A A9 D N.C. A+ D6
shoot-in' - est hoot - in' - est cow - boy a - round. Wood-y's Round - up.
4fr

YOUR HEART WILL LEAD YOU HOME

from Walt Disney Pictures' THE TIGGER MOVIE

Words and Music by RICHARD M. SHERMAN, ROBERT B. SHERMAN and KENNY LOGGINS

Original key: D♭ major. This edition has been transposed up one half-step to be more playable.

Em
Em(maj7)
A7sus
A
dif-f'rent and ev - 'ry - thing has changed. If you feel
D
D7
G(add9)
Gsus
3 fr
Gm
3 fr
lost and on your own and far from
Bm
F#/B
Bm7
2 fr
Em9
A7sus
A7
home you're nev - er a - lone, you know. Just think of your
Am6
5 fr
D7sus
D7
G(add9)
B♭6
friends, the ones who care; they all will be wait -

Bm7
2fr
Em11
7fr
Bm7
2fr
E7sus
E7
3
- ing there with love to share and your
3
Em7
A7sus
A7
1
Dsus2
heart will lead you home.
G6/9
D
A/D
Fun - ny how a pho - to - graph can
Am/D
G
Em7
D/A
A7
3
take you back in time to plac - es and em-brac - es that you thought
3

D7sus
D7
G
F#
you'd left be - hind.
They're try - ing to re - mind you that you're not
Bm
B
Em
Em(maj7)
the on - ly one that no one is an is - land when all is
D/A
A7
2
D
said and done.
If you feel
home.
Bm7
2fr
E9sus
E9
There'll come a day when you're los - ing your way and you don't

A7sus
A7
A/D
D
know where you be - long.
Bm7
E9sus
E9
They say that home is where the heart is, so fol-low your heart
Gmaj9
G
A7sus
A7
and know that you can't go wrong. If you feel
D
D7
G(add9)
G
Gsus
Gm
Lead vocal with choir:
lost and on your own and far from

Bm
F#/B
Bm7
2 fr
Em9
Em7
A7sus
A7
home, you're nev - er a - lone, you know. Just think of your

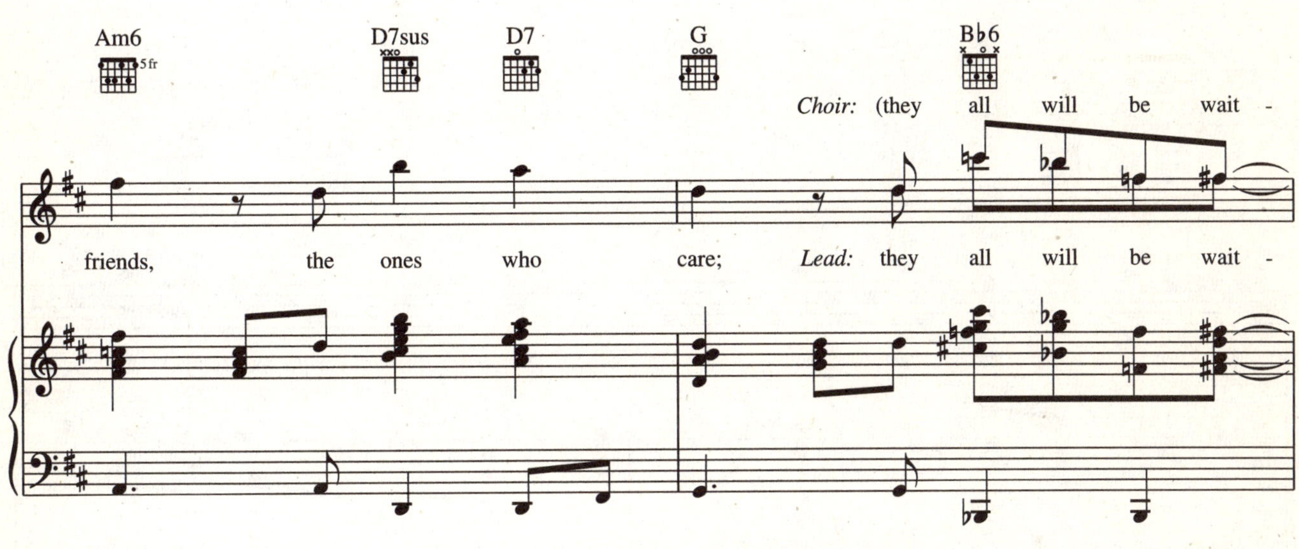
Am6
5 fr
D7sus
D7
G
Bb6
Choir: (they all will be wait -
friends, the ones who care; Lead: they all will be wait -

Bm7
2 fr
Em11
7 fr
Bm7
2 fr
E7sus
E7
- ing there.
- ing there with love to share. And your

Original tempo
Em7
A7sus
E
E7
Children: (Ooh,
If you feel
lost and on your
heart will lead you...
Lost and on your
rit.

A(add9)
A
Am11
C#m
G#/C#
C#m7
own and far from home,)
own and far from home,
Children with Lead Vocal: you're nev - er a -

F#m
B7sus
B7
Bm6
E9sus
E9
lone, you know. Just think of your friends, the ones who

A(add9)
A
C6
C♯m7
F♯m11
4 fr
Children: (they all will be wait - ing there.
care; Lead: they all will be wait - ing there with
C♯m7
4 fr
F♯7sus
F♯7
F♯m7
B7sus
4 fr
B7
love to share and your heart will lead you
Slower, more freely
Bm6
7 fr
E7sus
G9
F♯m11
B7sus
4 fr
B7
where you be - long. I know your heart will lead you
Original tempo
Esus2
Esus2/A
Esus2
Amaj13
E(add9)
home.
rit.

ZERO TO HERO

from Walt Disney Pictures' HERCULES

Music by ALAN MENKEN
Lyrics by DAVID ZIPPEL

G C/G G C/G G C/G
les. Whose dar-ing deeds are great the-a - ter? Her - cu -
G B♭ E♭/B♭ B♭ E♭/B♭ B♭ D7 Csus2/E
les. Is he bold? No one brav - er. Is he sweet? Our
6fr
6fr
Fdim7 D7/F♯ G G7/B C D7sus G G7/B
fav - 'rite fla - vor. Her - cu - les. Her - cu -
C D7sus G G7/B C D7sus G G7/B
les. Her - cu - les. Her - cu -

C
D7sus
G
G7/B
les.
Her - cu - les.
Her - cu -
G/B
Bless my soul, Herc __ was on a roll,
un - de -
Csus2/E
D7/F#
feat - ed. __
Rid - ing high, Spoken: and the nic - est guy.
Not __ con -
E♭7
F/G
ceit - ed. __
He was a noth - ing,
ze - ro, ze - ro.
Now he's a hon - cho,

F/G G F/G G D7sus B7 Em
he's a he - ro. He hit the heights at break - neck speed.
Am7 G/B C C♯dim C/D Am7 G/B C C♯dim
From ze - ro to he - ro. Herc is a he - ro.
C/D Am7 G/B C C♯dim C/D D7sus
Now he's a he - ro.
D G7
Spoken: Yes, in - deed.

YOU MUST LOVE ME

from the Cinergi Motion Picture EVITA

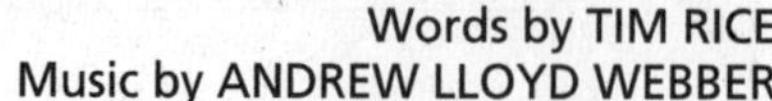

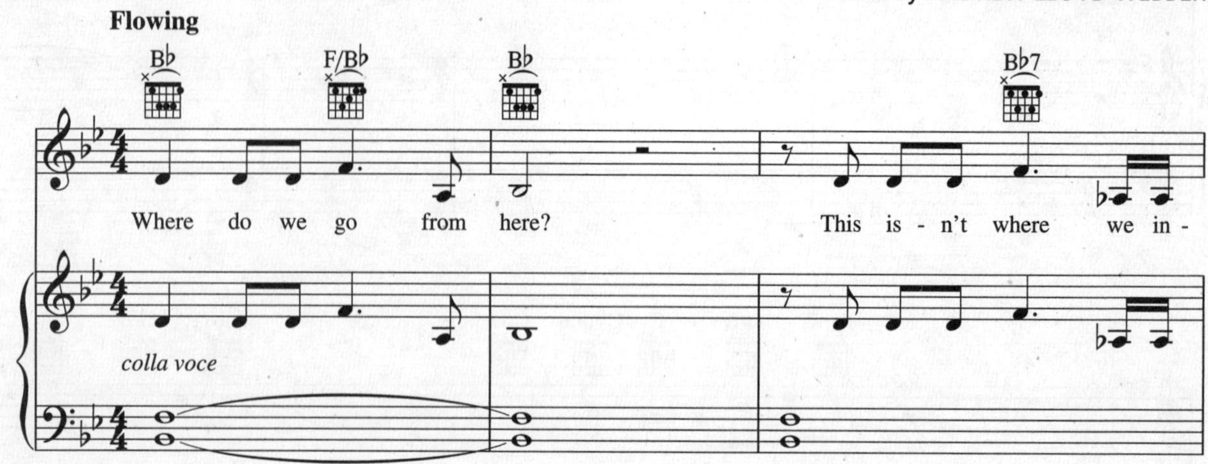

B♭ B♭7 E♭ 3fr
pear what do we do for our dream to sur - vive,
side? How can I be an - y use to you now?
Cm7 3fr F11 3fr F
how do we keep all our pas - sions a - live as we used to do?
Give me a chance and I'll let you see how noth - ing has changed.
F11 3fr F D7 Gm 3fr D7
3
Deep in my heart I'm con - ceal - ing things that I'm long - ing to
Gm 3fr D7 F/E♭ E♭ 3fr Cm7 3fr Dm7
say, scared to con - fess what I'm feel - ing fright - ened you'll slip a -
rit.

F
B♭
E♭/B♭
6fr
F/B♭
B♭
To Coda
way, you must love me,
you must love me.
a tempo
E♭/B♭
6fr
F/B♭
B♭
F/B♭
B♭
B♭7
E♭
3fr
Cm7
3fr
F11
3fr
F
F11
3fr
F
D.S. al Coda
CODA
E♭/B♭
6fr
F/B♭
B♭
You must love me.
rit.